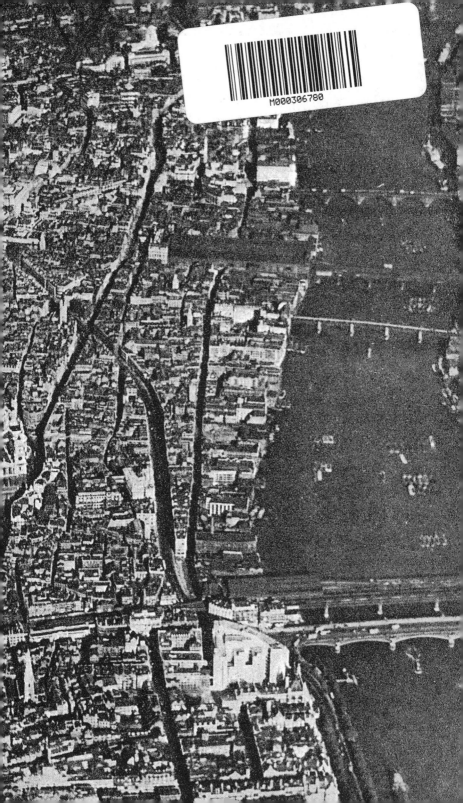

THE SPIRIT OF
LONDON

By

PAUL COHEN-PORTHEIM
Author of "England, the Unknown Isle"

With a Foreword by
SIMON JENKINS

Illustrated from Photographs

LONDON
B. T. BATSFORD LTD

First Published, February 1935

Reissued 2011

By Batsford
10 Southcombe Street, London W14 0RA

An imprint of Anova Books Company Ltd

The moral rights of the authors have been asserted

ISBN: 9781849940283

A CIP catalogue record for this book is available from the British Library.

18 17 16 15 14 13 12 11
10 9 8 7 6 5 4 3 2 1

Printed and bound by 1010 Printing International Ltd, China

This book can be ordered direct from the publisher at the website: www.anovabooks.com

FOREWORD

BY SIMON JENKINS

MY first London job required me to walk to work off the Strand through old Covent Garden market. It was a glorious initiation into the personality of the metropolis. I recall early winter mornings with freezing mist rising from hosed-down gutters, the smell of ancient cabbage, and the bizarre sight of nuns gleaning discarded vegetable scraps for their kitchens. I treasured those sensations in the sure knowledge that they would soon pass, and pass they did.

Far more has changed since Cohen-Portheim wrote his highly personal observation on London in the 1930s. He wrote of the horizon as of Wren's "city of dreaming spires", rising over a roofscape which the Victorians had not allowed to offend the majesty of St Paul's. He could write of a Thames whose flanks were swathed in the masts and rigging of sailing barges. His Fleet Street was still "the acropolis of the printing press." His London was still essentially English. It was not a city of tourists, indeed foreigners then found the place drab and "hopelessly boring". Ethnic enclaves were confined to just a few streets north and east of the City.

Yet leafing through Cohen-Portheim's pages, and especially his copious photographs, I find the continuity as startling as the change. Cities must live, eat and breathe, and they do so today much as they did between the wars. The fruit and vegetable market still opens and trades each morning, even if it is deep in the heart of Docklands, while its Smithfield sister battles on by Farringdon Road, stubbornly refusing to depart. As for old Covent Garden, it has acquired a new vitality and colour.

Most remarkable is how few of the views Cohen-Portheim depicts have been lost. The Museum of London once assembled footage of London streets as they appeared in the background of early movies filmed on location, fearing that a visual record might be lost for all time. Yet watching footage of cops and robbers in King William Street or a crooner on an open-topped bus, I was surprised at how recognisable most of the streets are to this day. The same applies to Cohen-Portheim's townscape.

Despite the bombing of London, the landmarks which he picked out are still with us. We have the old Mansion House and Lombard Street, The Mall, Piccadilly and Regent's Park. We have Shepherd's Market and Berwick Street, St Lawrence Jewry and St Martin-in-the-fields, the Coliseum and the Old Vic. Of the bridges, London and Waterloo

Bridges have gone, unnecessarily, but the rest have survived. Cohen-Portheim could today repeat his observation that the City's medieval layout of lanes, alleys and courtyards has survived to an extent unimaginable in most comparable business districts. Hardly any are even called streets.

The greatest transformation lies elsewhere, deep behind the facades, in Cohen-Portheim's fascination with London's people. Most publishers avoid people in guidebooks – and certainly pictures of people – as it tends to date them. No such inhibition restrained Batsford in 1935. An extraordinary number of the pictures in this book are not of London but of Londoners. Some are of urban functionaries, opening parliament, assembling the Lord Mayor's show or enforcing the law. But most are just anonymous crowds, on the loose in the city. They are engaged in watching a football match, strolling in the park, buying at a sale or waiting for a train. They are pictures of no one and everyone. They people the urban space with a personality rare in topographical literature.

We follow Londoners down streets wet with rain, enveloped in fog, noisy with horses and bereft of pavement cafes. We see them dive in and out of pubs, forced to retire home in the evenings when everything closes down. They gather easily in crowds, cloth capped or bowler hatted, grim or laughing. Cohen-Portheim lists the contemporary stars of theatre and music hall, Thorndike, Gielgud, Laughton, Laye, Cooper and Buchanan, and writers then in the ascendant, Shaw, Maugham and Coward. I note that the number of West End and suburban theatres (other than cinemas) he cites, approximately 100 in all, is almost the same number as would be listed today. We catch a glorious glimpse of Gracie Fields on stage from behind, singing out into the dark.

These Londoners had already come through what they regarded as the war to end all wars, and had experienced financial crash and depression. Their city had suffered much. But they were about to suffer far more, making this record peculiarly poignant. The war was to do more than blitz the East End. It broke up families and neighbourhoods and sent them scattering to the suburbs. The closure of the docks and much of London's manufacturing industry transformed the workplace and sucked in hundreds of thousands of immigrants from the provinces and abroad. If the buildings of London were to suffer only surface wounds in the years to come, the city's social geography was to be unrecognisable.

The more valuable is a work that does not pretend to be a guide but is rather one man's observation of London at a single moment in time. I know of few books that leave a more vivid impression of the city I love.

Simon Jenkins 2011

PREFACE

By RAYMOND MORTIMER

THIS book seems to me decidedly the best introduction to London that one could give to a friend from abroad. But he might reasonably complain that the warnings it contains are inadequate, that there is no other great city which so turns its back upon foreign visitors —food which is either expensive or tasteless, only one outdoor restaurant, two cafés (both remarkably ugly), and no night life except for the very rich. Before spending money on a *Come to England* campaign, it would be better to make England a pleasanter place to come to. Consider the London which the average Indian student sees, a London of bad-tempered landladies and cretinous tarts, with the Paris which welcomes the Cambodian and the Martiniquais, and you can hardly be surprised at what is so humourlessly called the disloyalty of the educated Indian.

Monsieur Paul Morand, whose wit, fancy and perceptiveness I very greatly admire, wrote a most flattering portrait of London, which was, however, disfigured by a number of surprising errors. There may be mistakes of fact in Paul Cohen-Portheim's book, there are certainly judgments with which I strongly disagree— in my opinion, for instance, he grotesquely overestimates the work of both Raeburn and Epstein. But he certainly would not have made August Bank Holiday occur on a Saturday, as Monsieur Morand does. For he was not only a good Londoner, he was a good Cockney. And there would always be a fag hanging down from his lip as he sloped along with the crowd. There was often also a camera in his pocket, and among the photographs in this book taken by him there is one, of a guardsman flirting in the Park, which is typical of what caught his fancy. His understanding of England was extraordinary; and indeed he had leisure in which to develop it. For in 1914 he was caught here by the outbreak of war, and after some months of persecution was placed in an internment-camp—an experience which he described in what is probably his best book, *Time Stood Still*.

This book on London was written in English: he intended writing it also, I believe, in French and German. For he was much more than a good Londoner, he was a good European. At present in every country, including England, there are powerful and malignant forces which deny the very concept of Europe. In Germany to be a good European is a crime punishable with imprisonment, exile, torture or death. The Roman Empire declined and fell largely because its citizens ceased to believe in it; and Europe seems destined for a similar fate. The arteries will again be cut as they were in 1914; the victim will bleed to death; and the surviving continents will cheerfully pass a verdict of *felo de se*. I am not suggesting that these other continents have nothing of value to contribute to civilization—Cohen-Portheim himself wrote of Asia with intense appreciation—and it is possible to hope that patriotism to Europe will in time be swallowed up in patriotism to the Earth. But if some intelligent Asiatic or African asks what grounds one has for one's attachment to the idea of Europe, I would suggest that it is only European tradition which combines the belief in reason, the belief in humaneness, and the belief in quality. And any *Weltanschauung* which neglects any one of these beliefs must be inferior, because by starving the brain or the heart or the senses it is denying man his fullest development. (l am not suggesting that Europe has ever lived up to these beliefs.) The devastating results of neglecting either reason or humaneness are clear in history. The importance of the sense of quality is less recognized, for until recently Europe has not suffered seriously from neglecting it. But anyone who has visited the United States knows what a civilization with no sense of quality is like. Mr. Aldous Huxley, in *Brave New World*, depicted a society eminently reasonable and humane, a society by utilitarian standards immensely good, showing an illimitable balance of pleasure over pain. But, lacking all sense of quality, it was not a Utopia, but a nightmare.

The premature death of Paul Cohen-Portheim is tragic not only to his many and devoted personal friends, but to those who share his belief in the concept of Europe. In itself it is a small thing to be equally at home on the Zattere and the Kurfürstendamm, in the Rue de Lappe and in Islington. But it is upon the spread of an attitude to Europe like that expressed in different ways by Norman Angell, Julien Benda, and Paul Cohen-Portheim that the continuance of civilization depends.

AUTHOR'S NOTE

THE author does not feel that a new book about London needs an apology. However lengthy the list of books on that subject may be, it remains as inexhaustible as ever; London is so great and so comple a pheno- menon, and it is moreover so constantly changing, that there is no reason why people should ever cease writing about it.

But if such a book does not need an apology it needs a preliminary indication of its character, for there are many imaginable categories of books on the subject. This book, then, does not profess to be a "complete guide-book," yet it hopes to guide. *A guidebook enumerates, this book appreciates.* A guidebook is obliged to give pride of place to the most famous sights or curiosities; this book takes them for granted. Where it mentions them; it is not in order to describe them but to explain them; it is a critical not a descriptive guide. A guidebook must be complete, that is to say, include all sorts of dull matter; this book does not profess to be complete, but to offer a choice of what—according to the author—is most remarkable, curious, or unknown in London. As it wants to *interpret* London, it is at least as much concerned with the *life* of London as with its buildings and officially recognised sights. That is, incidentally, why the photographs illustrating it are considered a very important factor.

The book contains, I think, a good deal of information not to be found in a guidebook, while it omits most of what the guidebook offers. It wants to convey the atmosphere and *spirit* of London; it is a book about what London stands for and what it means. It hopes to appeal not only to those whot while already knowing London slightly, wish to know it a little more intimately, but also to those who, while knowing it, like to be reminded of it; and yet to others who may perhaps never see it and would still like to feel they know it a little. If it should, as I hope, appeal as well to the Londoners or English themselves, many of whom must know it far better than the author, that would be because they might like to hear a foreigner's views on the sights and subjects so familiar to them, and thus possibly see them from a new angle.

As soon as a book of this sort ceases to be purely descriptive, and becomes explanatory or critical, it is bound to encounter opposition. Where the author states his opinion, the reader may think him wrong or ill-informed. But while prepared for this, I hope that there will be one thing no reader will deny, and that is that this book is written by one whose sympathy with London is very sincere, and who might, in fact, almost be said to be in love with it.

P. C.–P.

PUBLISHER'S NOTE

The contents of this book is a faithful facsimile of the original 1935 text. As such, it includes the phraseology of the time, including references to class and race, which may seem insensitive to today's audience. The opinions are very much those of the author and reflect the period in which they were written. We hope, however, that this is of interest to today's readers, but wish to remind readers that the writer's opinions are not shared by the Publishers, and no offence is intended. The book obviously includes descriptions of places in London in the 1930s, some of which have disappeared and some of the information in the book is now out of date. References to the 'last century' is to the 19th century.

LIST OF PHOTOGRAPHS

CONTENTS

2   LONDON DRIZZLE

3 ST MARTIN'S-IN-THE-FIELDS, TRAFALGAR SQUARE, FROM
THE NATIONAL GALLERY PORTICO

THE SPIRIT OF LONDON

CHAPTER I

LONDON THROUGH THE CENTURIES

No one knows exactly what London is, where it begins or ends, or how many people inhabit it. It is a city, a county, a postal district or a police district, and as it is ever spreading, growing, and changing its form, all these divisions do not embrace the whole. There is but one well-defined London: the City of London, and the City is both essential London and not London at all— essential because it is both its cradle and its centre, but not London at all because it is an administrative district independent of all the rest. The City stands, however, for historic London, and no capital gives one a more profound feeling of historic continuity—this in spite of the fact that it contains very few early historic remnants. In this it is very characteristically English, for the English are very practical business men, but at the same time devotees of tradition and of historic institution. As business men they are quite prepared to destroy a building or an institution if this stands in the way of progress, but as worshippers of the past they like to retain their name and semblance. Thus a street may be full of modern buildings, and have lost its old character, but it will retain its name, and therewith some of its memories. That is why few of the streets of the City are called "streets," while it is full of Gates, Markets, Lanes, etc. There is hardly an historic street in Paris that has not changed its name and hardly one in London which has. England is the oldest constitutional and parliamentary monarchy, but it retains all the pomp of feudal royalty, and in exactly the same way the huge London metropolis retains its City, with its Lord Mayor and Aldermen, its mediaeval guilds, its rights and privileges; and the King of England may only enter the City with the solemn if symbolical permission of the Lord Mayor. The houses

C

of the City stand on historic ground, the names of its streets are ancient, and—what is more remarkable—its ancient topography is almost unchanged. No Napoleon or Haussmann have here destroyed old quarters and drawn broad and straight avenues through tortuous mazes; the City is still a mediaeval rabbit-warren of courts, alleys, and passages, through which a few main thoroughfares stretch in winding curves and angles. In its lay-out the City of London resembles a Siena or a Lubeck, but its ancient houses have vanished, and in its buildings. it appears a modem business centre, full of offices, banks, and business premises. This is, however, a deceptive appearance, for hidden in odd nooks and corners are aImost innumerable vestiges of the past, if few of the early past. The City is truly a wood you cannot see for trees, and only, when you cross the Thames and gain a little of that distance the narrow streets deny you, will you discover its real character, that of a city of offices and warehouses surmounted by innumerable steeples and towers of churches, dominated by the huge dome of St. Paul's; and thus unique in character.

It is difficult to imagine the Roman City of London, for Rome has not left its stamp here as it has done in most other parts of its dominions. There are no traces of the logical and geometrical planning of the Romans, there are no remnants of their temples or amphitheatres; there remain but a few unimportant vestiges of masonry, and a bath. And yet excavations made a few years ago on the site of the Bank of England have proved that the business centre of twentieth-century London is the same as that of Roman London, so great is the continuity of this city—and so great its change which abolishes the traces of the past. There, as now, London's business centre was where Bank, Exchange, and Mansion House stand, and—if legend is to be believed—there as now the Deity was worshipped on the hill where St. Paul's stands. The London Bridge of to-day is but a successor of the bridge the Romans crossed to enter the City, but if they entered it they would find no trace of their city left.

The first period to leave visible signs on the face of the City was the Norman. William the Conqueror, who found the City already a self-governing body, which he confirmed in its rights and privileges, built his fortress, the Tower, just outside the gates, and there it still stands, still not included within the boundaries of the City, surrounded by a maze of later additions, and dwarfed by Tower Bridge. The Tower being London's most famous historic monument is naturally overrun by sightseers, and thus it is difficult to recapture the spirit of the past there, while being conducted in a herd by a uniformed shepherd. Besides that, its surroundings are all against it; it lies too low nowadays, the surrounding greenery is too pretty for its grimness, the bridge-towers dwarf the White tower; it is, in short, a "museum-piece" like so many famous sights, but not a living part of London's huge body. Its attractions are world-famous: armoury, regalia, beefeaters, and—last but not least—tragic memories, but it is not a spot I have ever wanted to revisit (except the very perfect chapel of St. John's), though I like to sit on the terrace, facing the river, where you may see people eating their sandwich-lunch, perched on absurd ancient pieces of artillery, and slum children playing about, while tugs and barges hoot and glide past, and there are no over life-size diamonds you are expected to admire, and no tiresome historical dates to remember. For some reason or other I can feel no interest in what remains of mediaeval London: it seems dead to me, and not connected with the living London of our day. St. Bartholomew's the Great, though incomplete, is a very fine example of Norman architecture, as is the round church of the Temple, but to conjure up a vision of mediaeval England one must go to places like Shrewsbury or Wells or York, where the past has remained part of the fabric of the present. And the same applies to Gothic London (Westminster is a thing apart), and even to the London of the Renascence; these periods have left vestiges, of course, but their spirit has departed, that spirit so very much alive still in cathedral cities and university towns, and in so many villages of

England. A few houses in Holborn and in the Strand show what the City must have looked like before the Great Fire, and there are some Gothic churches, among which I prefer the charming little Ely Chapel with its crypt; there is the Guildhall and there is the Charterhouse—if London were an "art-city" like others one would have to admit that it possesses many treasures of the architecture of those times, and go into raptures over them. But London is not Siena or Rothenburg, but a most enormously vital metropolis, and I consider that only that of the past which still lives belongs to it properly, and that the rest—no matter how beautiful—is not part of the living city but of a museum, the exhibits of which happen to stand in streets instead of in galleries. It is not the age of a building which matters most, but the degree to which it is representative of the city you wish to become intimate with. Every great city has a period, or possibly several periods, which put their stamp on it and determine its character; all that came before loses its significance, and all that comes after is no longer essential. While this is true of all ancient cities, it is quite particularly true of London, for London was destroyed by the Great Fire, and a new city arose in its stead.

The City of London is what the seventeenth century and Wren made it; it is a classical structure on a mediaeval plan, and if Wren's great reconstruction had been executed it would have been classical in every respect. It would have been far more magnificent, far more logical, and also far less typically English. As it stands, it is a very English compromise. Wren gave the City its new silhouette, built his extraordinary symphony of white spires round a dark dome, but in their shadow Londoners rebuilt their ancient maze, which they have preserved to this day; for no matter how many new buildings go up —and ever so many are going up at present—they cannot change its essential character. It is because Wren's churches had to remain hidden in narrow alleys that he gave all his thought to the spires, and as a result the City possesses what no other city in the world can show: a co-ordinated group, a harmony of all its church spires

4   THAMES' SHIPPING IN THE UPPER POOL

5   THE DOME OF ST PAUL'S AND THE SPIRES AND STEEPLES OF THE CITY

conceived by one master-builder. Truly here for once it is right to speak of a symphony in stone. This symphony, and not this historical monument or that, is the great art treasure of the City, and a very little-noticed treasure it is! True it has not been entirely preserved, for high modern buildings have spoilt the original proportions in many places; but one can still appreciate it from the other side of the river and more particularly from the top of St. Saviour's tower, and it is without doubt one of the great architectural wonders of the world. In order, however, to appreciate Wren's genius fully, one should examine the spires and churches at close quarters. How extraordinary is their variety and how extraordinarily original is the English interpretation of the classical Renascence! While all the details belong to the classical alphabet, the general impression produced by these churches is romantic, picturesque, northern. These spires are all romance, and more truly "dreaming" than those of Oxford. St. Bride's is like a pagoda, St. Mary-le-Bow, St. Clement's, so many others all variations of the same theme: a romantic and picturesque effect achieved by classical and severe means. It is a very rare harmony of elements that would seem incompatible, and this extraordinary achievement is as characteristic of Wren's genius as his failure to build the towers of Westminster Abbey in "the Gothic style"—they are more uninspired than the nineteenth-century Gothic of the Houses of Parliament.

Henceforth the classical spirit ruled the City's architecture. Somerset House, the Mansion House, the Bank, Waterloo Bridge, the Royal Exchange, erected at very different periods, are all one in spirit and tradition; and a simple and more domestic classicism is also the dominant note of the residential parts of the Temple and the other Inns of Court. It is not their earlier churches or halls which determine their aspect, but the long rows of simple and perfectly proportioned deep-red brick houses. Classicism in its peculiar English variety is the dominant architectural note of the City. It is a place of Victorian offices and banks, inspired by Renascence palaces and black with soot, intermixed with historical vestiges and Wren churches and classical halls, out of which grow in ever-increasing number the huge white office-blocks of the twentieth century. It looks as if the City was trying to "grow up" in rather too much of a hurry, especially in its centre, where all the big banks have started on the upward path. If you examine it in detail, you will find it composed of any number of incongruous parts; but there is one strong dominant note which no amount of carelessness and indifference has been able to destroy.

The first part of what is now London to be added to the City were the boroughs of Southwark and of Westminster. Southwark has its priory church, now the cathedral, to attest its age, which suffers from lying below the present street-level, and has been very much restored. A fragment of one of the famous old inns has survived, but it seems strange to think that in Shakespeare's time it was the centre of stage life and probably of "gaiety," for now there are nothing but warehouses and wharves, slums, and a few broad thoroughfares of no great character. But if you forget about the houses and tUrn your attention to the population of this district your impression will be quite a different one, for "The Borough" is full of a popular life, very characteristically English (infinitely more so than the East End), and of a roughly humorous vitality, very Shakespearean in quality. The "Elephant and Castle," surely one of the ugliest traffic centres in the world, is surrounded by theatres and music-halls, the public and the spirit of which are undoubtedly much nearer Shakespeare than those of West End theatreland. Melodrama still lives here, the music-hall still resounds to the chorus taken up by all the audience, and I do not think it an accident that the "Old Vic," the modern temple of Shakespeare, should lie near by.

Westminster is as rich in monuments of the past as Southwark is poor. Its wonderful Abbey and its palace, originally remote from London, were gradually joined

6   SUNDAY MORNING IN LOMBARD STREET

7　BELGRAVIA: Belgrave Square

8　BLOOMSBURY: Bedford Square

up to it by a series of riverside palaces, all of which, with the exception of Somerset House, have disappeared. Only names like the Savoy or Norfolk Street still recall them. Of the greatest of these, the Royal Palace of Whitehall, only the banqueting hall survives, probably the best Renascence building in London. Even the royal residences of London seem to change their aspect continually. St. James's Palace retains its old gate-tower, but little besides, and Buckingham Palace turns a new façade to the world. Growth and change refuse to be arrested. Already prudent, Queen Elizabeth had thought that London was getting beyond itself, and interdicted further growth, but for once she did not have her way. A very important factor in its development was the absence of any danger of attack after the victory over the Spanish Armada. Whereas the great continental capitals remained fortified, and their growth was restricted by walls, painfully pushed farther out from time to time, London could spread at ease, and in any direction it liked. Not only that, but it could afford to build low houses, one-family houses, and thus its character changed entirely. Elizabethan London was not strikingly different from the Paris of the same period, but the London which arose after the Great Fire was quite unlike any continental city, except the Dutch ones, which developed on similar lines for similar reasons. London swallowed up village after village, district after district, and grew formless and indefinite. People ceased to live in the City as they got to appreciate the advantages of space and air. I think that the Dutch influence on English architecture and town-planning, possibly due to some extent to William of Orange, is much greater than is generally recognised. Holland had evolved a very high culture of the bourgeois or citizen type, in which it led the world in the seventeenth century. There had ever been a close connection-due to the Hansa—between Holland, Flanders, Northern Germany, the Baltic, and England; it ceased when the Hansa died, but in the seventeenth century it reasserted itself again, artistically and culturally at least, under Dutch leadership. In Paris or Vienna the great nobles and a very few rich men lived in houses, or rather palaces, of their own, the rest being crowded into high tenement-houses, as they still are; but the wealthy burgher of Amsterdam had his own house, narrow-fronted and of dark brick, with spacious rooms, full of solid dark furniture, pictures, and silver, and, last but not least, with its own little garden, in which he lived his unostentatious but very comfortable life. It is that type of house and that manner of life which now conquered London. The architecture was modified and simplified; London did not take over the Dutch gables; the spirit here was more severely classical, and English architects invented the square and the row or terrace, grouping units which alone seemed too insignificant into a larger and more impressive whole. Thus arose the characteristic architecture of London's huge residential quarters, which was to remain practically unchanged for centuries, and which has given it an aspect entirely different from that of the other great European capitals. Nor did it continue to resemble that of the Dutch cities, for London did what they—being so much smaller—had never thought of doing: it radically separated business quarters from residential quarters. Tudor London had lived in the City in the continental manner, Georgian London made a business centre of the City and lived outside it. The West End grew up' as the dwelling-place of the wealthy, and London housed the less well-to-do and the poor in houses smaller but similar in type in the East, North, and South. Huge districts became covered with large (though not very large), medium-sized or tiny one-family houses, built of brick, red, yellow, or greyish. Mostly they grew up where and how they pleased, but now and again an attempt at town-planning or at a comprehensive architectural scheme was carried out, generally due to the initiative and sense of a big landowner who had decided to develop his property. Bloomsbury is such a conception of the late eighteenth century, laid out in straight streets and squares; the Adelphi is another; but by far the most important is Nash's bold planning and building from St. James's Park up to Regent's Park. Later there came Belgravia, and other minor yet sharply defined planned oases in the general confusion.

Victoria's reign was very long, and London's growth during that period phenomenal. As it went on swallowing up villages and towns it retained or built in each a main street, devoted to business and shops, while the rest became residential. Thus London ever seems to come to an end and ever begins anew. Hammersmith follows Kensington, Fulham follows Chelsea, Hendon Hampstead, and so on, on all sides, until you think that the sequence will never end. Perhaps the most typically Victorian residential districts are Kensington and Bayswater. There has been no radical departure from earlier domestic architecture, but brick has gone and stucco (already since Nish) taken its place; the houses are heavier, the proportions less good, and in all directions stretch endless rows of monotonous "pillared porticoes." Wealthy merchants build large square stucco villas on the hills of Sydenham, where the Crystal Palace (once more admired at present by the modern of moderns) found a final resting-place, and a ring of stucco suburbs grows around London, to be followed by the pseudo-Gothic or pseudo-Tudor suburbs of later years, the newer, and the newest, while the older go out of favour and decline from respectability, as cars and tubes replace horses and Metroland arises.

Some of the newer suburbs are well laid out and prettily built, like the Hampstead Garden Suburb; some are indifferent and some shoddy; but the upper classes despise them all indifferently, and their dwellers prefer to call them dormitories, for "suburban" is a term of reproach or derision. I think this extremely silly, for on the whole London has every reason to be proud of its suburban development, which a good many German cities, for instance, are imitating at present. True, their architecture is indifferent, often bad, but what a very pleasant, healthy, and clean existence in fresh air they procure for literally millions of people, who in continental cities would have to live cooped up in tiny flats or tenements! They have pretty gardens, they have decent accommodation for the children, and the rents there are quite extraordinarily low. What a contrast to the London slums!—though certainly the latter are more picturesque. There are many pleasant natural features, too, in vast suburbia: commons and heaths, rivers and hills, so that even a sightseer could do worse than visit them; but their great appeal will be to sociologists— and to politicians.

Nearly all great public buildings outside the City are Victorian. Some of the earlier are still classical in charac- ter, like the British Museum or the National Gallery; some are samples of the Gothic Revival, like the Houses of Parliament, the Law Courts, or St. Pancras Station; and most of the later ones, like the Kensington museums or the Whitehall Government Offices, are more or less successful adaptations of Renascence styles. Most of the theatres were built then (and even the older ones rebuilt), and the big hotels sprang up around Charing Cross; the Strand and Northumberland Avenue are still the centres of hotel life, theatre life, and night life, which stretches as far as Leicester Square, where the old Empire and the Alhambra were at the height of their glory in Victorian and Edwardian days. There is the Academy, there are the clubs of Pall Mall, there are many banks. Pall Mall represents the best of the Victorian tradition; it is an English version of a street of Italian palaces, dignified, spacious, immensely solid, and a little gloomy.

As ever, the character of the sovereign and of the period are akin, each great sovereign becoming a symbol of his time. This was a patrician epoch, stately, if inclined to be pompous; solid, if inclined to be heavy; impres- sive, if liable to be depressing. Just now it is the fashion to deride it, but that will pass. The Albert Memorial is indeed very funny, but the Houses of Parliament and the Carlton Club (both architecturally and symbolically) are distinctly impressive, and they are undoubtedly very typically English. And without doubt the Victorian spirit is still predominant in England, as Victorian

9   LOWER MIDDLE CLASS: Tooting

10   UPPER MIDDLE CLASS: Wimbledon

11   A SUBURBAN DORMITORY IN SURREY: Sanderstead

architecture still predominates in the appearance of London. Both are intensely English, and they were born at a time when England was further removed from the Continent and from foreign influences than it has been before or since. The London of Dickens and Thackeray was very much more distinct from the Paris of Balzac or of Zola than that of Aldous Huxley from that of Jean Cocteau, and the Prince Consort did not much resemble Napoleon III. The rapprochement—political as well as cultural— took place during the short reign of Edward VII. Unfortunately, architecturally that was about the worst period in European history, and the London architecture of that time is no exception to the rule. Everything becomes bombastic, over-decorated, insincere. There are cupolas and statuary, and there is much marble and gilt, and every building is a sham palace. Fortunately for London, this was not a time of great architectual activity, as it was, for instance, in Berlin. The Y.M.C.A. in Tottenham Court Road, the Wesleyan Hall opposite Westminster Abbey, the Gaiety Theatre—to name but a few of my pet aversions—are pretty representative, but they do not equal the Berlin Reichstag and Siegesallee, nor the Paris Grand Palais. The one good piece of work of that time is the Mall, very Parisian in inspiration, but finished off—alas!—by the white wedding-cake of the Victoria Memorial.

In after-war years the building activity of London has been very great, and it is difficult to keep pace with it. You find work of all qualities: good, bad, and in-different. There are excellent modern buildings, like Adelaide House, Olympia, the Underground buildings; there are many with incongruous bits of historical styles tacked on somewhere; there are especially among the cinemas—some abominations. Much that is valuable is being destroyed, but also much one is glad to see dis-appear. Whole districts are changing their character, and everywhere flats are replacing houses. London is in the midst of a transformation, as it always has been, and always will be while it is alive. And it is marvellously alive, and it is the old which has remained alive that we have been following through the centuries and trying to describe. For in London the past—at least a very great deal of the past—is not dead; the City is alive, and alive its Abbey and its Cathedral, and its Georgian squares and Victorian clubs and houses of legislature or law. As alive as the very latest white concrete cube or super-cinema, and as much of the present as of the past.

12   MORNING IN THE MALL

13   EVENING IN PARK LANE

CHAPTER II

TOWNS WITHIN TOWN

For some obscure reason, the wealthy quarters of nearly all capitals are situated west of the centre, but nowhere is this tendency more marked than in London, where to the smart or rich the idea of living anywhere but in the West End would seem fantastic. And this residential West End wanders ever farther west, while business and the entertainment industry encroach on it from the centre. Covent Garden, Lincoln's Inn Fields, Russell Square have in their turn been the heart of the West End; St. James's Square followed, and at present Grosvenor Square and Berkeley Square fulfil that august function, though probably not for much longer. They are the heart of Mayfair, and Mayfair is the heart of the West End, or at any rate its smartest and most distinguished quarter. Unlike some other quarters, Mayfair has sharply defined boundaries; it lies between Park Lane and Bond Street, between Oxford Street and Piccadilly. In London the very poor and the very rich alone have the privilege of living quite close to the centre of their activities; the inhabitants of Mayfair live just around the corner from the smart shopping streets, Bond Street and its surroundings, the smart hotels and restaurants, the Parks, and not far from the clubs of St. James or Pall Mall; Whitehall, Westminster, and theatreland. If it pleases them, it is easy for them to walk to any of the places likely to play a part in their daily life, for this "smart London" is really a very small town, and it is the existence of such small towns with a character of their own which distinguishes London from other capitals. Here people of like social status as of like professions like to crowd together to the exclusion of outsiders, and thus to live in a small town of their own which alone to them is "London." The British are aristocratic by nature, or snobbish, if you prefer to call it that; that is why an address is a matter of great

E

importance, for here an address is a label. In Paris people belonging to the same social class or set may live in almost any quarter, but not so in London. There are a few historic mansions in odd corners, a few originally minded may elect to live in Bloomsbury or near Regent's Park, but Society in its great majority has decided that Mayfair is the proper place to live in if you are one of its members. True, there is early nineteenth-century Belgravia, there are the terraces of Carlton House, the houses facing the Green Park; there are Portman Square and Portland Place, but none of them can rival Mayfair, for Mayfair alone is a *symbol*. "Mayfair" means the place where the mysterious great live, in whose doings the less great are so vastly interested that their newspapers are filled with them. Duchesses reside here and viscounts, and also (though the suburbs disapprove) American and Jewish millionaires, but an ordinary person has no business here. The sins of Mayfair's smart set have inspired countless playwrights and novelists, and probably it is quite enough to call a book or a play "Mayfair" to sell it! Mayfair is one of those golden symbol-words which make millions of people tremble with delight—like Ascot, Cowes, Eton, or Oxford. Most of these millions would probably deny this imputation—but look at the space these symbols take up in print!

What does this social paradise actually look like? I confess that I do not find it particularly exciting and would not "reside" there even if I were a multi-millionaire. For one thing, it is quite flat, and its planning is uninteresting. Its show places are the two squares and Park Lane; its other streets are quite nice if rather narrow, and it has masses of twisting mews, where expensive cars have replaced expensive horses, and one picturesque enclave: lowly Shepherd Market. Many of its houses are dignified seventeenth- or eighteenth-century mansions, but London has never built palaces in the grand manner of Rome, Vienna, or Paris. These houses are larger than the average houses of their times, but otherwise similar, and the few really important mansions left,

14   GEORGIAN HOUSES IN QUEEN ANNE'S GATE

15   REGENCY HOUSES IN PARK LANE

16   MAY MORNING IN PICCADILLY

17   SHEPHERD MARKET, JUST BEHIND PICCADILLY

such as Crewe House and a few others, look to me like country houses out of place. But even without comparing Mayfair to the corresponding quarters of foreign cities, I think other quarters of London far more beautiful. It has neither the grand unity of conception of Nash's terraces, nor the distinguished charm of the Bloomsbury Squares; not even the rather heavier distinction of Belgravia. It is the fashion to say that Mayfair evokes the eighteenth century, and to mention Walpole to show your familiarity with its historic atmosphere, but to me its atmosphere seems late Victorian, and, still more, Edwardian—not historic, but pre-war. For though it certainly holds other memories, that period surely saw it, and all it stands for, at the height of its glory. Then there were great hostesses, great receptions in great houses, and the impressive carriages of the Lansdownes, the Westminsters, and the Marlboroughs could still be met with in the neighbouring park. But at the same time "smartness" and "fastness" had already been invented, and had replaced the "grace" of the eighteenth century and the "dignity" of early Victorian times; and it is the combination of the dying grand and the rising smart manner which made "Mayfair." People had already begun to appreciate the charms of hotel and restaurant life; they had already admitted new elements—millionaires from new countries or of alien races—to their sacred precincts; they had begun to become slightly "naughty," but Mayfair was still a purely aristocratic preserve, still a sacred city.

But it has ceased to be that now, and its character and aspect are changing very rapidly. The symbol still retains its magic, but it no longer corresponds to reality. Mayfair is becoming the Champs-Élysées quarter of London, a place of luxury hotels, huge blocks of expensive flats, and very smart shops; and as it is small in size, change here is not gradual, but rapid, and there is not so much conversion as demolition. The first shops still kept to a few streets, the first hotels grew up on the borders: Ritz, Berkeley, and Claridge's. Mayfair's passing began when Devonshire House (incidentally a rather grim and forbidding mansion) was demolished, and a huge hotel arose and overlooked Berkeley Square. Thomas Cook came, Berkeley Street changed into a more modern Bond Street (the prettiest modern shops of London are here), and Berkeley Square is about to follow. It is sad that Lansdowne House has gone, but what it stood for went when its old owners and neighbours departed. There are flats in Grosvenor Square, though they do their best not to look like it, and Park Street is nearly all flats nowadays. But the greatest change has come over Park Lane. Two enormous hotels now bear the names and stand on the sites of Grosvenor and Dor- chester Houses, and they symbolise the change which has come over Mayfair (and incidentally over all the world). Mayfair is still a place for the rich, but for the rich of all nations and of no matter what origin and ancestry. It has ceased to be the Faubourg St. Germain of London and is fast becoming its Champs-Élysées, so far as London's far less cosmopolitan character allows. Hotels, flats, cars, and cocktails are rapidly destroying its character. Many mansions survive yet, and there are a few streets the modern spirit has left untouched, like Clarges and Half Moon Streets, which ever since the eighteenth century have been the home of that peculiarly English type: the young man about town. Shepherd Market is still a market and full of vegetables and funny old public-houses, but many of the mews have become pseudo-cottages, and the grand old plane-trees of Berkeley Square shudder at the thought of a new shopping-street which will soon run along them. Things have changed indeed, but I don't see why one should weep over it. Life is far more interesting than stones, and Mayfair is expressing life and the changing social conditions. Perhaps the plane-trees (and other delicate souls) might be comforted by the thought that a good many of the Mayfair shops are run by descendants or relatives of the owners of the big houses, or else by Russian princes in exile. They will have to get used to modern Mayfair and to the fact that nowadays there are not very many women left whose chief function is to be "seen in the Park" or "looking lovely" at Covent Garden or elsewhere, and few men whose sole occupation is attending races or shooting big game; and if they observe these people a little closer, they will discover that most of them are not really descended from the Crusaders at all (I mean the original, not the "Empire" variety). It may console them to think, however, that there are still quite a number of aristocrats left in England, though their names do not appear in the gossip columns; and anyway they really need not worry more about this particular Ichabod than the people who are personally affected by it, for while these may dislike the change, they would in all probability dislike it far more if they were obliged to live the lives of their noble ancestors of a few generations ago, who "could afford it."

You need only cross Piccadilly to leave Mayfair for St. James's, and you will come to a London where time has stood still, though it is not quite easy to say exactly when it decided to do that. It takes its name from the Palace, which replaced a hospital, and of which little that is old survives except the very charming clocktower. The Court of St. James's, to which ambassadors are still accredited, has elected Buckingham Palace for its residence, but levées are held there, and there is nearly always some conference sitting which assembles the political leaders of Europe, the British Empire, or the world. But though St. James's is called after the Palace, it does not take its character from it. It is a very curious island, surrounded on two sides by parks and on the other two by rivers of modern life: Piccadilly and the Haymarket. Between them lies the real St. James's, centred around St. James's Square, which has changed a good deal since the seventeenth century which saw its birth. St. James's is clubland and the home of the bachelor. It is a rich and luxurious quarter, but its wealth and luxury are of a peculiarly English kind, and there is nothing in the least like St. James's in any other capital. The "chic" quarters of Paris, for instance, are far more impressive than those of London, but no one would dream of calling St. James's chic (what a blasphemous thought!), and Paris could not have produced it, for it knoweth not clubs. Pall Mall and St. James's Street are not the only club streets, for there are many clubs in Piccadilly, and scattered about the West End, but they are the typical and ideal ones. Pall Mall received its character in the early nineteenth century, when the classical club-palaces arose which are frequently called gloomy nowadays. I disagree with this verdict, for they have a dignity and spaciousness about them which I admire. They are certainly neither "gay" nor *gemütlich*, but then they were not meant to be substitutes either for Montmartre or for middle-class homes. Architecturally they are classed as "Victorian," which is historically correct, of course, but spiritually absurd; they are classical in spirit. Napoleon is not unthinkable in them, and I am certain Goethe would have felt quite at home in the Athenaeum, and admired its library, classical frieze, and statue of Athene—I am certain of this, because Goethe's own house in Weimar looks like a miniature Athenaeum. The whole street is one of the finest in Europe, but personally I prefer St. James's Street, because I prefer the eighteenth century to the Early Victorian period. St. James's Street has some clubs housed in most perfect eighteenth-century build-ings, amongst which my favourite is Boodle's, with its charming windows, a perfect building of Adam type, though Brooks's runs it pretty close. But St. James's Street has other things to show besides clubs. It is the "High Street" of the island city of St. James, and St. James's is a masculine paradise, the home of the male half of Society, of the man of fashion. It provides all he needs: lodgings and flats, all that belongs to his dress (though the male centre of fashion stretches beyond its borders), his ties and shirts, shoes and hats. London is the only capital in the world that has a masculine fashion centre (it is the world capital of masculine fashion); in Paris the mere male has no place that belongs to him, nor has he in Berlin or Vienna; his adornments are sold amid the far greater feminine splendours of the Rue de

18   BOODLE'S CLUB, ST JAMES'S STREET

19   CUMBERLAND TERRACE: A Stucco Group overlooking Regent's Park

20   THE ATHENÆUM CLUB, PALL MALL

la Paix or the Linden, the Champs-Élysées or the Kurfürstendamm, but in St. James's he rules supreme. The elegance of St. James's is entirely masculine, and it is inimitably English. It is subdued, never showy; it goes for quality, not for effect. Much, very much has changed in England, but St. James's still exhibits what people abroad mean when they call a thing English, and inform you in reverent whispers that a tweed, a pair of shoes, a pipe, an umbrella, a hat, or a suitcase are *echt englisch* or *vient de Londres* (the reverence with which women all over the world regard the creations of Paris forms an amusing parallel). By this they mean that the article is solid, is the very best of its kind, perfect in finish but with an unobtrusive perfection which only the connoisseur will recognise. Such are the goods of the famous hatters, umbrella-makers; such the pipes, port, and tobacco of St. James's, famous all the world over. In fact, I think that both continentals and Americans get far more excited about these products than the English themselves, who take them as a matter of course, for familiarity breeds contempt.

It is the well-dressed man who dominates St. James's, and he is astonishingly similar to his ancestors, the beaux of old who trod the same pavements. But like those ancestors, he is a good deal more than well-dressed; he is a man of culture. The very peculiarly aristocratic culture of England is mirrored in St. James's, with its faultless but conservative taste. St. James's is a centre of art, but of old, well-established, and recognised art only. You will see magnificent Chippendale chairs and cabinets, Chelsea china, and perfect mezzotints, Queen Anne silver, and Chinese porcelain; you will see pictures by the great painters of Italy and Holland, by Reynolds and Gainsborough—but you will look in vain for a Picasso or the products of the Bauhaus Dessau. True, you may find motor-cars or even aeroplanes in St. James's Street, but you will find state-coaches shown in the windows of a shop surely unique in the world, and in all St. James's you will not find anything eccentric or anything cheap. You will find a few very fashionable

restaurants, small, expensive, and unobtrusive. St. James's
does not know what it is to advertise, and does not wish
to know; it despises electric signs and leaves its shop-
windows in decent darkness at night. It is not only
not modern but anti-modern, but it is not old-fashioned
either, for that only is old-fashioned which was modern
yesterday. But St. James's stands for something very
English of all times: it expresses the ideal of a city for
English gentlemen, for Englishmen of leisure and taste
and breeding. That ideal varies in some externals, but not
in essence. The man you meet in St. James's to-day is
differently dressed to his predecessors, he drives a car
instead of horses, and he may have to make a living;
but in character, looks, and in all essentials he resembles
and carries on the traditions of his ancestors, as his sons
and descendants will resemble and carry on his traditions. St. James's is conservative England, but conservative England at its best.

You do not have to go far from St. James's to find
different worlds, for the West End is as varied in itself
as the whole capital of which it forms a part. It is so
varied, in fact, that one can only pick out a few of its
more remarkable components, describe but a few of its
"islands." Across the Green Park from St. James's, just
across the road from Mayfair, lies BELGRAVIA, which
ranks second to Mayfair socially and architecturally. It
dates from the beginning of the nineteenth century only,
which is why it does not rank as high in public estima-
tion as Mayfair with its seventeenth- and eighteenth-
century traditions, but it has retained the character of a
purely residential aristocrats' quarter while Mayfair has
almost lost it. Belgravia is quiet, on the grand scale, and
somewhat depressing. Its centre, Belgrave Square, is
an impressive ensemble of spacious stucco classicism;
Eaton Square is almost too long to be called a square,
but it has distinction, and so have all the streets of that
well-planned and uniform district of pillared pale yellow
family mansions. Belgravia is impressive and slightly
alarming like a dowager duchess. It knows no shops or

21   NEW HALL, OLYMPIA: The Floodlit Front

22   STORE LIGHTS IN BROMPTON ROAD

23 BATTERSEA POWER STATION FROM THE RIVER

trade except on its outskirts, and one feels almost an intruder there if one has no business in one of the mansions or embassies which compose it. It is quite an island, but it is not large, and a very few steps will bring you to the bustle and cheerful vulgarity of Victoria. VICTORIA is not really a quarter, it is a centre and a very lively one, too. It is one of the most puzzlingly planned or rather unplanned parts of the West End, a jumble like the agglomeration of railway stations from which it takes its name, and which hide behind big hotels, cinemas, and shops. There is a motor-bus station wedged in between the railway stations, and a modernist motor-coach station near by, and so it is ever crowded with hurried people departing or arriving; and if no one seems to have any business in Belgravia, everyone seems to in or at Victoria. Two large cinemas and a music-hall fit themselves into the puzzle somehow, and the pavements are always full of soldiers from the many barracks close by. Victoria Street, which starts here, lives up to its name, and is truly Victorian (of the 1860-80 variety), immensely solid and full of worthy "emporiums" and rather black and respectable, but it hides the astonishing Westminster Cathedral, and leads straight to Westminster Abbey, where a new world begins. All the roads from Victoria lead to different worlds, and you may choose between Vauxhall Bridge Road and its shabby-genteel Pimlico district, Grosvenor Gardens, which will take you to Knightsbridge, where you will find Piccadilly continued in shops and hotels, where you will find Harrod's and old curio shops and smart women shopping and the twentieth century, or else you may take one of several streets which lead to Chelsea.

CHELSEA is at least two places: fashionable Chelsea and old Chelsea. The former adjoins Belgravia, and became fashionable in the later part of the nineteenth century. It has a huge square, Cadogan Place, and many red-brick, more or less Tudor houses spreading westward. From the pale yellow stucco classicism of Belgravia you emerge into gables and brick and terracotta, from pillars to what was "modern" about 1890, but Sloane Street

F

is a street of very up-to-date shops, if not of modern
buildings, and the inhabitants of this part of the world
are quite of the twentieth century. Sloane Square is
where it ends and where the real Chelsea begins, which
is one of London's most delightful islands. It is very full
of history and memories, but also very full of life, so
you can take your choice. It lies between the Thames
and King's Road, and the king who built the road was
Charles II, who found it necessary for his many visits to
Nell Gwynne. Thus Chelsea has a somewhat amorous
origin, and that may account for its having been for so
long London's "Bohemia." To Charles Chelsea owes
its Palace, the "Hospital" of the red-coated veterans, so
decorative in Chelsea's streets, and its beautiful gardens.
Chelsea is associated with poetry and art and philosophy.
Carlyle lived here and has his statue. He was a most
unpleasant husband, but perhaps Chelsea air is bad for
husbands, for Rossetti was an eccentric one, and Whistler
'and George Moore remained bachelors. I suppose
Chelsea as a centre of art was at its height in the 'nineties,
when Whistler immortalised its river-mists, and it became
aesthetic and artistic and Bohemian. That is when all
those old curio shops sprang up, and those with art-
pottery and art-curtains, and people started to paint
their doors in strange and bright hues. There are many
older remnants of older periods, of course: lovely Queen
Anne houses facing the river and a pleasant old church;
the Herb Garden and that of the Apothecaries', where the
Flower Shows are, and Crosby Hall, which does not really
belong here, and any number of odd little corners and
cottages and squares; but it is the 'nineties which gave
Chelsea its atmosphere. It suffers from that fact at present,
for if it is still an artistic centre it is not that of present-
day art, even though Augustus John has remained faithful
to it, who is the chief representative of modern painting
in the eyes of the British public, as Epstein is of modern
sculpture. There is a slightly "arty" flavour about
Chelsea which the younger generation of artists dislikes,
and which has driven it away. Rossetti and Ruskin,
Whistler and George Moore have stamped Chelsea, and

that gets on the nerves of post-impressionists. But it is a good place to live in, with or without art, and pleasant to saunter along the river and see barges and bridges and the trees of Battersea Park, and the new monumental power-station opposite, and the four huge chimneys which guard Chelsea's frontier.

From the Royal Borough of Chelsea it is not a far cry to the equally Royal Borough of KENSINGTON, which is, however, more respectably royal in origin, owing that distinction to Dutch William's Kensington Palace; and if the Restoration is responsible for Bohemian Chelsea, perhaps that model couple, William and Mary, have for ever imbued Kensington with an aroma of affluent respectability. There is a huge district which goes by the name of Kensington, but the only true Kensington is that of the Palace, Gardens, High Street, and Square of that name, and a very charming small *Residenzstadt* it is. Palace and Gardens are pure if simple baroque, the square and side-streets are full of eighteenth-century houses, Edwardes Square is a pleasing oddity, but yet Kensington is pre-eminently Victorian. You must watch it in the High Street, that very busy shopping centre with its huge bazaars which seem always to have "Sales" on. High Street is as purely feminine as St. James's Street is masculine, but they belong to different centuries and classes. Kensington is very wealthy, but it is not at all smart; some of the largest and finest houses in London stand in Palace Gardens, but Mayfair would not care to live in them. Kensington is patrician rather than aristocratic, it belongs to the rich bourgeoisie, it is the home of the "Forsytes," and it is the Forsytes you see in its streets, their well-dressed children and prim nurses that you will meet in the Gardens. I have always felt that Kensington ought to erect a statue to Mr. Gladstone (even though the Queen objected to him), it seems so "old-fashioned Liberal." Perhaps it has simply remained rather Dutch, and the Dutch are admirably patrician.

The "Greater Kensington" includes London's museum

city, which I consider one of its greatest missed
architectural opportunities: half a dozen huge and costly
buildings utterly unrelated to each other! There is also
the Albert Memorial, justly considered a joke, and the
Albert Hall, which should not be considered one, for
it is magnificent. (Victorian things are mostly one or
the other, and sometimes both.) It includes the Brompton
Oratory, a fine Italian Baroque building which always
looks continental and out of place, bordered by two
charmingly absurd country cottages leaning against a
former tube-station, and deliberately hiding an Anglican
church behind it—quite a characteristic London jumble.
There are the great stucco-cliffs of Queen's Gate, whose
massive walls mostly house "boarders" now; there is
Holland House, a beautiful country house in the midst
of London; and there is Leighton House, a real Royal
Academician's dream. There is Campden Hill, where
Kensington aspires to art, and there are enormous
districts which all go by that name, though their decayed
gentility bears but the faintest resemblance to the rock-
like patricianism of the real Royal Borough. But if
Kensington fades away into shabby fringes on some
sides, it more delights if you follow its High Street, for
it will take you to HAMMERSMITH, which has charms
ancient and modern. Its ancient charm is the Mall
alongside the Thames, one of the spots where that
erratic river allows you to walk along it and get a proper
look at it. The Mall is sacred to booklovers, for it is
the home of the Kelmscott and the Doves Press; besides
that it is full of curious little cottages and charming old
houses, and you may walk as far as Chiswick Mall with
yet finer houses and a still better river, and realise that
Pope, Walpole, and Tree had good reasons for electing
to live there. The modern charms of Hammersmith are
varied. There is Olympia, the new part of which is one
of the best modern buildings in London, the great
exhibition hall of England where the Horse Shows and
the Motor Shows are held, and the Royal Tournament
and the great circus at Christmas, and where you may
gaze at "Ideal Homes" even if you can't afford to own

24   THAMES-SIDE SUBURBIA: An Air View of Kew and Chriswick

25   ACADEMIC INTERLUDE AT THE BRITISH MUSEUM

26   UNIVERSITY COLLEGE, GOWER STREET: The Luncheon Interval

27, 28   SUN AND SHADOW IN THE TEMPLE: Middle Temple Hall
and Fountain Court

29 SOHO: Berwick Market

one. There is the Lyric Theatre of *Beggar's Opera* fame, and there is the Palais de Danse where one now skates, but which is still beloved of the youths and maidens of London who are not wealthy but yet fond of entertainment.

And when you have tasted the delights of Hammersmith go on to Putney and walk on its wide heath and common, where you will forget that London is still all round you and fancy yourself in the country, and go on to Kew and the most perfect gardens in Europe. Fit in Fulham and its palace somehow, and go even farther to Richmond, its terrace and its park, lose yourself amongst the oaks and the deer, and imagine you have at last left London far behind—which you have not.

If instead of travelling towards the west and the south from St. James's one turned towards the east and the north, one would find quite as many surprises. A few minutes' walk takes one from traditional, English, cultured St. James's to Soho, which is its opposite in every way. SOHO'S only tradition is that it is a foreign quarter, for it appears that when it was laid out in the late seventeenth and early eighteenth centuries many of the wealthy Huguenots, who had fled from France after the revocation of the Edict of Nantes, settled in that new and fashionable district. But if Soho is still foreign, almost entirely so, it is certainly not a fashionable residential district, but a curious continental enclave in London's shopping district. It lies between the big shops and the theatres, between Regent and Oxford Streets, Charing Cross Road and Shaftesbury Avenue, a foreign island in London waters. There are not a few such foreign domains in London, but Soho is the only one in the West End. Its streets are straight and regular, most of its houses specimens of the excellent domestic architecture of the eighteenth century. Its main square has a number of these left, amongst which is a charming structure in its south-western corner which was once the Venetian Embassy (where Casanova is believed to have stayed), and might almost stand in Venice. It has

fortunately been preserved, but a good many others
have been replaced by taller modern offices, so that
the general aspect of Soho Square is mixed. But it is far
from unpleasant, and can look surprisingly beautiful at
night when the cross on its Italianate brick church
stands out luminous against the dark sky—the only
ecclesiastical use of a sky-sign known to me in Europe.
Golden Square is almost entirely rebuilt; its houses are
of all sorts of sizes and ages, so that it looks rather like
a family of big and small, older and younger brothers
and sisters. But Soho is not famous for its houses, but
for its foreign restaurants. Its population is largely
Italian, intermixed with French, and there has been a
large Jewish influx in latter years. The Jews are connected with the clothes and fashions—cheap but up-to-
date—of Berwick Street and Poland Street, but most of
the other foreigners must be connected with the numberless French, Italian, Spanish, Chinese restaurants and
little cafés of Soho. Soho has one of London's most
entertaining street markets, in Berwick Street, and all
that neighbourhood is full of foreign grocers, bakers,
and butchers. The very mixed foreign population has
spread beyond the Soho boundaries and conquered New
Compton Street and Charlotte Street amongst others.
Greeks, Armenians, Cypriots, and Negroes have haunts
in the former, while in the latter flourish more French,
Italian, and German restaurants and *Delikatessen* shops.
If Soho restaurants attract people of all classes, Charlotte
Street has an artistic clientele, for Fitzroy Street, which
continues it and leads to the grand Adam houses of
Fitzroy Square, is full of painters (attracted there by the
great old rooms which make perfect studios), and they
may be found forgathering in a tavern there. If you
add to all these varied elements the film, which has its
headquarters in Wardour Street, you will understand
that Soho is one of the most picturesque and entertaining
quarters of London. It is full of noisy children, barrel-
organs, and street singers, Italian waiters, shady indi-
viduals of both sexes and of many races intermixed
with people in faultless evening dress; of funny little

paper shops which exhibit *Il Secolo* and *Le petit Parisien* amidst cards of *belle chambre meublée a louer*, and others where you see cheap finery or Chianti bottles or waiters' outfits. No bus passes through Soho; the roaring traffic of London only skirts its boundaries, and in this it is an island like St. James's. But it is as thoroughly cosmopolitan as the other is thoroughly English, and only in London could you find a foreign quarter so untouched by the spirit native to the city which surrounds it and another so English and untouched by the modern cosmopolitan spirit.

Between the West End and the City, and properly belonging to neither, lies BLOOMSBURY, bordered by New Oxford Street and Euston Road, Tottenham Court Road and Southampton Row. It is famous as an early example of town-planning, a city of straight streets and of many squares, and architecturally one of the finest parts of London. Its houses date mostly from the eighteenth and early nineteenth centuries, the best period of domestic architecture in London, for that is when the type of the English one-family town house had matured. No modern architect could improve on their strict simplicity; they achieve their effect by perfect proportion only, and they are full of charming fireplaces and ceilings and staircases. Bloomsbury was built as an essentially patrician quarter, but it has changed its character more than once, and is changing it again at present. For London is not content to leave old quarters for newer and more westerly ones, but it may take it into its head to set fashion flowing backwards, to "reclaim" districts already abandoned, which is what is happening to Bloomsbury.

The heart of Bloomsbury is the British Museum. That probably began its transformation into a visitors' district. I don't think there can be as many hotels in so restricted a space anywhere else in the world, and quite certainly not as many boarding-houses. Not expensive hotels nor smart ones, but still less "commercial." They cater for a peculiar class of visitors or more permanent

inhabitants, because it is the Museum and University
College which dominate Bloomsbury. It is full of book-
shops and publishers' offices and all sorts of societies
and Oriental art shops, and it is a *quartier latin* of learning,
but emphatically not of gaiety. Gower Street is full of
Indian students, who have their club there; professors
and learned people from all over the world fill the
hotels around the Museum. But Bloomsbury has a mixed
population, and it is not all learning. The countless
boarding-houses shelter that typical human assortment
so amusingly portrayed in Munro's play *At Mrs. Beam's;*
they are full of "genteel" old ladies, of "retired" people
of all sorts who cannot afford a home, of young clerks
from the Continent trying to learn English, while in
the summer they and all the available accommodation of
Bloomsbury are submerged by the tide of American
tourists of the non-wealthy but "cultured" kind who
wish to visit the Museum, the Abbey, and Dickens' Old
Curiosity Shop. They like the prim teashops of Bloomsbury, and its art and handicraft galleries, its temperance
hotels, and its "old-world atmosphere." When, however,
modern London talks of "Bloomsbury" it is not think-
ing of transatlantic visitors nor of the Elgin marbles, but
means a certain intellectual set, the members of which
live, or have lived, in that district and made it famous
again in the last twenty years. That Bloomsbury is a
"highbrow" place—that is to say, a very influential intellectual centre. The "Bloomsburies" have had a decisive influence on modern thought and art in England,
and this Bloomsbury is to-day to a very great extent
Chelsea was in the 'nineties. Clive Bell is the
prophet of modern art in England, Duncan Grant the
most prominent post-Cézanne painter there, Keynes
perhaps the most influential economist. There is Leonard
Woolf who edited the old *Nation,* and his wife, Virginia
Woolf, one of the great novelists of the age; there are
writers like Victoria Sackville-West, critics like Earp or
Raymond Mortimer, sculptors like Dobson, composers
like Constant Lambert or Walton, to name a few rather
at random. "Bloomsbury" influences the universities

and the reviews, parliament and politics, publishers and papers. It is a very important factor in present-day England and not a very well known one. It is proud of its (intellectual) island status, and exclusive; it does not desire popularity. It is not the home of best-sellers nor of much-boomed celebrities. It is on the other hand a link or borderland between art and culture and that Society which in England has ever been their patron, and is so even now. It likes to think that what it admires to-day the masses will worship to-morrow, and it is probably quite right.

The ADELPHI is not unlike Bloomsbury on a small scale. It is also situated between the West End and the City, dates from about the same period, and is equally connected with literature. Its situation between the Strand and the Embankment is one of the pleasantest in London, and it has the advantage of perfect architectural unity, as it has been left almost untouched since the brothers Adam built it. The Adelphi is almost hidden by its large and gloomy neighbours, and its existence is menaced by the Charing Cross rebuilding scheme. I am inclined to agree with Mr. Bernard Shaw that the "hideous" railway-bridge there is one of the very best in London, for I like its simple straight lines and its dark red colour. Shaw should know, for he lived many years in Adelphi Terrace, with Barrie for a neighbour, and has had time to get to know the surroundings. Adelphi Terrace is a perfect piece of eighteenth-century domestic architecture, while the Royal Society of Arts behind it is a perfect example of a public building of that period. It would be a very great pity if all this were to go and be replaced by blocks of offices. The terrace has charming views and not a few memories; there is the Savage Club, the many publishers' offices and societies, the Little Theatre to show that the Adelphi is not dead but a spiritual refuge in the very centre of bustle. There is the Adelphi Hotel, one of London's very few old hotels of character, and there are the gardens. Also, quite near, the Savoy Chapel hides behind the disdainful back of the Savoy Hotel, in the hope of being spared. Really, this little island between the buses of the Strand and the trams of the Embankment should not be allowed to disappear!

Fortunately there is no need to be anxious about the future of the near-by TEMPLE, that other oasis which excludes traffic and noise, though nowhere else in the world would you find such a one in the very centre of business life, where every square yard of ground is worth a small fortune. It is a legal fastness which its proprietors well know how to defend, for have they not stuck to it ever since it passed into their possession (in 1608 definitely), after having been in that of the Templars and the Knights of St. John? It is a strangely peaceful place, a kind of legal monastery; it is also a museum of architecture, from its Norman round church and the great Hall where Shakespeare acted to its rows and courts of dignified brick of the seventeenth and eighteenth centuries, and its incongruous and Victorian stone. It has trees and a fountain, and dark passages and gateways, a large square where many cars park to remind you that the Law does not ignore the present, and a dusty ancient wigmaker's shop to show you that it does not forget tradition. Lincoln's Inn and Gray's Inn are brothers to the Temple. LINCOLN'S' INN shows you real Tudor and pseudo-Tudor and all that lies between them, and it faces on the Fields of its name, with the most magnificent plane-trees in London, where you will find young people playing tennis and a modern monument (to Mrs. Ramsay MacDonald) which is not an eyesore. GRAY'S INN is perhaps the loveliest and certainly the most intimate of the three. Its great avenue was once a centre of fashion, and is now quiet like its calm brick courts. It was its Elizabethan chapel and its Hall where again Shakespeare faced the public; it was long the residence of Bacon, and if he really "wrote Shakespeare" he could certainly not have found a better place to do it in.

These, then, are the enviable islands of the Law;

30 ADELPHI TERRACE

31 PALL MALL CLUB

32 ROYAL SOCIETY OF ARTS, ADELPHI

34 CLIFFORD'S INN

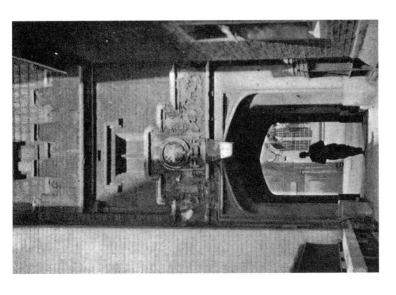

33 DEAN'S YARD, WESTMINSTER

35 WINTER IN WESTMINSTER

but the Church, too, has its island at Westminster, and it is perhaps the most perfect of them all. WESTMINSTER ABBEY itself faces the roar of London, but behind it lies strange peace, of all the ages. You may gaze at a Roman sarcophagus found there, at cloisters and lawns or at the Gothic chapter-house which held the very first parliament, or stroll on to the precincts of Westminster School, where the great tower of Westminster Palace overlooks the seventeenth and eighteenth centuries. You may even venture as far as the adjoining streets, Great College Street, etc., and go as far as Smith Square before you rediscover the present in the shape of huge offices, and slums in the process of being reclaimed.

Here I would like to add a few kind words about the Victorian Gothic Revival, for in spite of its detractors the Houses of Parliament manage to harmonise very perfectly with the Abbey, especially with Henry VII's Chapel, and they happily incorporate Westminster Hall. I like the effect of little white St. Margaret's next the large dark Abbey, like a tiny white yacht trying to race a four-master, and it does not detract from the character of the Abbey, for that is a jumble which is typically English. Contrast the Abbey and Notre-Dame of Paris, and you will contrast the character of the two nations. Notre-Dame is perfectly symmetrical, the Abbey absolutely irregular; the former is restored to its original purity of conception, the latter added to and changed about through all the centuries. Notre-Dame is perfect, very cold, and rather dead; the Abbey is most unequal and very alive; the former is a cold grey, the latter a warm brown. The nave of Notre-Dame is empty, that of the Abbey overcrowded with monuments, good, bad, or indifferent. Notre-Dame's chief glory is where you would logically expect it: its West front, while the West front is the Abbey's worst feature. The Abbey is a jumble, growing like nature in that haphazard English way which shocks logic and charms imagination. Henry VII's chapel is an incongruous addition, but also the Abbey's crown jewel. Ceiling and flags, Torrigiani's monument and the stalls, combine to form a picture of fantastic beauty nearer Moorish or Persian art than to that of Europe. How absurdly pedantic to limit "good architecture" to the severely functional!—art begins where that ends. Cloister, chapter-house, all the rambling surroundings of the Abbey are full of charm, but its greatest is the pageant of history it represents: Edward the Confessor's throne on which all kings have in their turn been crowned; all those kings and queens peacefully united resting there; all those Gothic, Victorian, or Baroque statues—down to the tomb of the Unknown Soldier.

This is London's most peaceful and quietest spot, quieter than any other capital knows; but if you wish to see that London holds the noisiest as well, transfer yourself from Westminster to Whitechapel, and visit PETTICOAT LANE and its immediate environment, and Sunday is the best day for this pilgrimage. You will find the Lane not only alive, but teeming, swarming, screeching, and bellowing on its market-day. Here is the most picturesque Ghetto of western Europe; all inscriptions are in Hebrew or Yiddish, the old inhabitants retain their dress of Russia or Poland, the younger are gaudily elegant, and all are immensely busy and boisterous. It is possibly the most surprising of the countless and ever-varied London districts, a few of which I have here described.

36   LONDON'S JEWRY: Aldgate, by Petticoat Lane

37 LUDGATE CIRCUS AND ST PAUL'S

CHAPTER III

STREETS AND THEIR LIFE

F<small>EW</small> cities have a greater number of interesting and notable streets than London, and certainly none has a greater number of monotonous and featureless ones. It is the only great capital built on the system of the small one-family house; that is why, when you get away from the central parts, you find acres of streets of undistinguished little houses, with only here and there a street of shops and business to interrupt their monotony. On account of this system London is a healthier, quieter, and pleasanter place for the masses to live in than continental capitals, but it is also responsible for the dull aspect of most of its outer residential parts. In a way that very dullness has a mysterious charm, and I find it fascinating to wander through those endless streets, alleys, terraces, and squares, and to wonder what people and what dissimilar fates those monotonously similar houses may hide. People of one class tend to crowd together, but there is little in the outward aspect of many districts to show what particular class inhabits it. All the older residential quarters are moreover interspersed with slums, so that only the modern suburbs are without diversity of life and hold no secret.

The number of streets notable in one way or another is very great indeed, in spite of the infinitely greater number of "anonymous" ones, and one can but mention a few of the most interesting. Every capital has streets the very names of which instantly conjure up a definite picture or convey a certain atmosphere, and it is these I call the "interesting" streets and am concerned with here. Many other very well known and important thoroughfares do not fall under this heading.

T<small>HE</small> C<small>ITY</small>, for instance, possesses next to none; it is too tightly packed for that. It is a warren round a central, absurdly small *place*, with probably the most intense traffic in the world. This is a small classical triangle,

H

surrounded by the Mansion House, the Exchange, and the Bank, which has now grown up to dwarf it still further. Round it are narrow streets, narrower lanes, courts, and passages—it is as one whole that one remembers the City, one does not think of its separate streets. The picture conjured up is one of a medley of grey banks, offices, pillars, columns, red buses, white steeples, and a seething mass of predominantly masculine humanity, all outcrowding each other. I find the City a cheerful place in spite of its predominant greyness; it looks so solidly prosperous, so immensely busy, and withal not at all hysterical. It is not even really rushed at "rush hours," it is just an uninterrupted but calm stream, and it is most fascinating to watch the human masses pouring into this cramped receptacle from railway- and tube-stations and over the bridges, or to see it being drained. Certainly no other European capital knows such immense crowding and traffic, nor does it know such uncanny emptiness and quiet as that of the City at night or on Sundays. It is only on Sundays that one can see the buildings, the background of the picture, the churches and little churchyards, the huge new white offices, and the streets, but this is like seeing a stage-setting without the actors, for the City is (to the unconcerned spectator) a show, a play, when it is at work, a play which begins and ends punctually, is repeated every weekday, and of the greatest human interest. It is the life of the City which fascinates, and it obscures its streets. Piccadilly Circus is sometimes called the centre of the world, but to me the City seems infinitely more deserving of the name, for it really is one of the centres of the world, that of finance and business, which dominate the times. The very houses show this—all these banks of Shanghai or Canada, of India or South America.

The City ends abruptly at Aldgate and the EAST END begins, which is one of the most mysterious places in the world, but of most prosaic aspect. It has none of the picturesque squalor of Belleville or the Faubourg St. Antoine; it looks mean and drab, and this impression is chiefly due to lack of height in its buildings. Apart

38   ALDGATE PUMP

39   WATERCRESS BARROW

40, 41   THE CITY: Kerbstone Activity in Throgmorton Avenue

42   LONDON BRIDGE: The Morning Influx of City Workers

43   RUSH HOUR: A mild struggle for a northbound bus

44 A CITY CHURCH INTERIOR: St Lawrence Jewry

from the great main roads it is just a maze of alleys of low little houses of darkened brick; nor can the main roads claim any distinction. Two endless roads traverse it under various names, the Commercial Road which leads to the docks and the Mile End Road farther north, and now and then a hospital, a church, a People's Palace raises its head over the dull low houses. It is the people who give interest to the East End streets. The Londoners do not love the street as the Latins do; they vanish into their houses, and there are very few streets where people "parade." There is, in fact, no equivalent term for the French *se promener dans la rue*. But if there is no term, the East End does "promenade" all the same; the West-Ender needs a park, but the East-Ender lives in the street. I do not know whether this is due to his love of the street or to the lack of comfort and charm of his home; probably it is due to both, but certainly there is joy and gaiety in the life of the East End roads. One explanation of this is the preponderance of the foreign element, amongst which the Jews predominate, and these Eastern Jews adore the life and light, bustle and noise of their WHITECHAPEL ROAD. On Saturday nights, particularly, it is thronged with people parading up and down; there is, in fact, a *Corso* in progress. I know of nothing quite like it in the more purely English popular parts of London, yet I have observed it in some big provincial cities of the North of England. Certainly the Whitechapel Road, with its smartly if cheaply turned-out girls and the youths with their gaudy scarves and caps, does remain in one's mind as one of the "pictures" associated with the name of a street, just as does "Petticoat Lane." LIMEHOUSE CAUSEWAY, on the other hand— "Chinatown"—is disappointing; its population is certainly Chinese, but they wear European dress; there are a few shops and restaurants. Probably there is some opium-smoking going on, but that or anything else of interest happens behind closed doors, and as a street Chinatown is a failure. Nor is the neighbourhood of the DOCKS as interesting as one would expect. There is no large and general picture of a seaport to be seen here, such as Hamburg or Marseilles offer. Each dock is separate and enclosed, and you must get a permit if you want to visit their fabulous warehouses and see the shipping. Nor will you find a "St. Pauli" or a "Vieux Port" life here; there are bars, amongst them the famous "Charlie Brown's," ship-chandlers, sailors' homes and institutions, but the sailors seem to take their pleasures elsewhere.

One sees much more characteristic popular life in other parts of London than in the East End. The ELE-PHANT AND CASTLE is a very live spot, for instance, with its pubs and cinemas, street markets and theatres, thronged with a good-humoured working-class crowd at night; and much the same life is to be found in ISLINGTON HIGH STREET, with the addition of a curious "northern" breeziness in the air. It is that kind of thoroughfare, the "Main Street" of a populous quarter, which is so typical of London; and there are heaps of them, because London is a mosaic of little cities each with its High Street, and the majority of their popula-tions do not travel to the centre of all things for their pleasures, still less for their shopping, but are content with their own little centre of life. "Main Street" has its inevitable cinema, often a theatre or a music-hall as well, and it has its pubs, its shops, its market, and street-stalls, and its crowd, not always sober but ever good-humoured. There is no greater contrast than between the prim respectability of a London middle-class suburb and the roving jollity of populous "Main Street," both equally removed from the smart and measured gaiety of the West End. It is the different character of the classes which make London life so very varied; and its "low-class" life is certainly not the least attractive, and without doubt the most cheery.

Leading from the borders of the West End to remote suburbs there are a number of "Super-Main Streets" which attract not only the local population but visitors from afar. Of such is the EDGWARE ROAD, which begins in great style between Marble Arch and the "Regal." It has cinemas and a theatre, pubs and street-walkers,

45   A LONDON "MAIN STREET": Evening at Camberwell Green

46   A ROAD IN WEST KENSINGTON

47   A STREET IN WHITECHAPEL

48   BARGAINS: King's Cross

49   BARGAINS: Islington

50   BILLINGSGATE MARKET

and on Saturday nights it seems to be the paradise of kitchenmaids and soldiers. It is straight and endless, and fades away into respectability and suburbs. In the south-west, VAUXHALL BRIDGE ROAD has a similar character, mixing soldiers and pubs and theatres and vanishing into semi-slums; but perhaps the most amusing of such roads is TOTTENHAM COURT ROAD. It begins in a narrow defile between the rival splendours of the "Dominion," faced by the "Astoria" where you may dance as well as see "the pictures," and Lyons' marble palace, which is indeed splendour for the masses. "Funfair," alas ! has gone, but there is a galaxy of cheap cinemas of the nice pre-talkie and even pre-war kind, peepshows, fried fish shops, and cafés. The crowd is varied; there are many foreigners of many colours, and of all London's streets of amusement it is most like a Parisian street of the same kind. It leads a double life, for if its nights are "pictures" and "corner-house:" its days are devoted to furniture—for from the great houses of Maple's or Heal's down to the smallest second-hand furniture shop, every house seems devoted to "bedroom-suites" or "chesterfields," and "Sales" never cease. It has a motley crowd by day as by night: Negroes from the purlieus of Charlotte Street, Indians from adjoining Bloomsbury, passers-by on their way south to the West End or north to Hampstead; and architecturally it is just such a medley of expensive if not beautiful huge twentieth-century erections, and low and dingy old houses, and stolid Victorians.

London's great centre of gaiety is, of course, the neighbourhood of PICCADILLY CIRCUS and LEICESTER SQUARE, too well known to need description. It is unsurpassed in Europe in its crowding together of numberless theatres, cinemas, and restaurants, in a very small space; it is a brilliant spectacle at the hour when all the theatres at once disgorge thousands and thousands of well-dressed people into the streets, and almost as many cars struggle in vain for freedom, while the sky-signs jump up and down hysterically. If you mention Shaftesbury Avenue, the Circus, or the Square, that picture

I

will spring up in the memory of everyone who knows
London, but I see no need to dwell on it, and my reason
is not that it is too familiar, which I think no reason at
all, but that I do not think it characteristically Londonish.
That kind of life and that kind of picture you will find
in all great capitals, with very little indeed to distinguish
one from the other: cars, evening-dress, and sky-signs
are exactly alike all the world over. It is only on the
nights of great football matches or of the Boat Race
and like events that these streets become unlike their
continental counterparts and bear some resemblance to
the unfashionable and slightly intoxicated merriness of
London, South or North.

The poorer parts of London are at their brightest at
night, when work has ceased; those of the well-to-do
during the day, for when shops close—and they close
early in the West End—most of their streets fade into
darkness. The West End boasts some streets whose
names are only mentioned with bated breath. Londoners
like specialisation, and some of their streets specialise in
one trade in a manner reminiscent of the days of mediaeval
guilds. These streets confer rank on the goods sold in
them in a manner unknown elsewhere—with the possible
exception of the Rue de la Paix—much in the same way
as some residential quarters enhance the social prestige
of their inhabitants. Chief among them is Bond Street,
and it comes as a surprise to strangers. Regent Street
is a wide thoroughfare with dazzlingly new, if not
beautiful, buildings; Oxford Street offers a sequence of
huge stores, and both look as you would expect the
most prominent shopping streets of a metropolis to
look; but Bond Street is a narrow lane, and its houses
are, with very few exceptions, small, old, and without
character. Bond Street is made by its shops and by its
public, but the shops again may surprise one unused to
London's notion of distinction, for they are mostly
small and old-fashioned, or at least not strikingly modern.
There are many modern shops and bazaars in London,
and one can see plenty of marble, glass, bronze, and
indirect lighting—but hardly in Bond Street, for all that

may be all right for shops which need advertisement or wish to attract the masses (Drage's in Oxford Street is one of the best examples of the kind), but Bond Street disdains advertising. Nor does it arrange its shop windows particularly well. You have to look a little closely, and then you will discover that nearly every one of these shops bears a name of world repute, and you will find the most famous art-dealers, jewellers, cigarette manufacturers, leather-goods shops, etc., in impressive sequence. Bond Street means quality—and the prices which go with that—and "bought in Bond Street" is their guarantee. The street is at its brightest before and after lunch, its life begins late and finishes early, and it is really itself only during the Season when it is crowded with all the people from England and from abroad who can afford to buy its goods. Then it is a street of well-dressed women and super-smart men with a characteristic swinging gait you never seem to see elsewhere, and a procession of expensive cars, occasionally varied by a carriage drawn by marvellously groomed horses, in which sit old ladies with remarkable Victorian hats. It is crowded and busy, but yet leisurely, for all these people are idlers. It used to be a boundary of the strictly residential Mayfair, but its spirit has now extended its domain west as well as east, and conquered the adjoining streets: Grafton, Bruton, Dover, Albemarle Streets, and Berkeley Street, which has become a serious rival. It has conquered Hanover Square, now a stronghold of dressmakers in the east, and is now threatening Berkeley Square in the west.

PICCADILLY, where Bond Street begins, is probably London's most famous street after the Strand, yet it has less character than some of the lesser known—or perhaps one should say that its character is mixed. It is always rebuilding, ever changing its aspect, but never loses a certain briskness peculiar to it. It is a neutral territory between female "Vanity Fair" and male, which overlap here—between Bond Street and St. James's. Its glory is, I think, not in its shops; they are first class, but not unique. Piccadilly is too "public" for that, too

much everyone's street. The last big store of Regent
Street marks its beginning, but after the Piccadilly Hotel
and a few shops, Burlington House (and St. James's
Church on the opposite side) interrupts business. Then
the shops begin again, but amongst them you do not
find *the* shop of any kind (except possibly Fortnum &
Mason's), not *the* hatter, hosier, etc. "Bought in Piccadilly" means nothing in particular—so Piccadilly soon
gives up trying to compete with Bond Street and tries
other dodges—hotels, for instance. It faces the Ritz with
the Berkeley, and you can't do better than that—but
then Claridge's, the Savoy, the Carlton are not here. It
throws out a cliff of luxury flats, isolated in their doubtful
glory, but next it stands the low old Bath House, looking
rather grim, not revealing the splendours it contains,
and, in fact, turning its back on Piccadilly. Then the
street changes its character altogether: on one side is
the Green Park, with its wide vistas and trees, on the
other are clubs, from the martial "In and Out" to the
diplomatic "St. James's"; but it never goes the whole
hog like Pall Mall, for a large new hotel interrupts the
clubs, while a second hides in a club building; then
there are a few shops again. Finally Piccadilly broadens
out like the mouth of a stream, ceases to be a street
without becoming a square, and ends in that vague
space known as Hyde Park Corner, with its alarming
one-way traffic circus. To the south lies a triumphal
arch surmounted by a top-heavy piece of sculpture, to
the north a row of large private houses ending in the
classical severity of Apsley House, spoilt by its sooty
columns and flanked by the graceful entrance gate of
Hyde Park. Piccadilly is sometimes straight and sometimes crooked, sometimes level and sometimes up-and-
downhill, and for some reason it is always cheerful in
a way very few London streets are, and one of a very
few West End streets alive at night by virtue of the
traffic it carries to and from the theatres and restaurants.

I confess that I have no great liking for REGENT
STREET, not because I deplore the disappearance of the
old, for its houses were dingy and had long been spoilt,

51 THE LIGHTS OF PICCADILLY CIRCUS

52   BOND STREET

53   THE STRAND, FROM TRAFALGAR SQUARE

54   THE NEW REGENT STREET FROM THE AIR

55   REGENT STREET: The Quadrant from Piccadilly Circus

but because the new seem very cold to me—for an all-white street does not suit London skies, it belongs to Paris. Its architecture might, it is true, have been worse, for at least some little unity has been preserved, but how much better it might have been! Regent Street reminds me of a woman whom people describe as "really admirable" because she is worthy, but none too attractive. It has very good shops, but no outstanding ones except the unique Liberty's; its crowd is well-dressed but not smart; it is spacious, but it no longer gives an impression of great width since its buildings have grown high. Especially the Quadrant has lost that quality. I find Regent Street curiously reasonable, but without charm; it is London's Avenue de l'Opéra, while Bond Street is its Rue de la Paix. Nor am I very fond of OXFORD STREET and its "ladies' mile." It is an impressive assembly of huge stores and drapers' shops, but it has a strangely suburban or provincial atmosphere, and always seems full of agitated spinsters holding hands while trying to cross the road, and red-faced stout women with many parcels bumping into everybody. Perhaps, however, its main defect as a street is that it has no beginning and no end, and just runs on for ever under varying names. I think the more westerly shopping-streets much more attractive. KNIGHTSBRIDGE is, and Brompton Road which continues it. It always comes as a surprise to find all the bustle starting anew after Hyde Park Corner, where any other city would decide to begin villadom. I like the Hyde Park Hotel towering over small old houses, the red mass of Harrod's which is a shop with an aura of infinite solidity, and the fascinating row of old curio shops, with stone lions and sarcophagi standing on a pavement reached by steps amid a few absurd trees. After that the Oratory, so surprisingly Catholic, and the Museum City begin a new world. I approve of SLOANE STREET, which has a feeling of modernity about it, and of a type of women who shop thereabouts, who are smart though not necessarily grand or millionairish, like they are (or should be) in Bond Street. These streets do not depend

K

so much on the "Season"; the people you meet here seem to live in and belong to that part of the world, and you feel that quite possibly some of them can't pay their bills. There is nothing stolid about this neighbourhood; it is a "young" place in spirit, and it also has the advantage of not being a "sight."

In all but the last characteristic its very opposite is HIGH STREET, KENSINGTON. Its charm consists in the contrast between its aspect and its public. It begins (as another surprise) after the calm of Kensington Gardens, and you are at once in the midst of it. A huge hotel (with lovely views and a famous chef), half a dozen very large modern stores, a town hall, a church spire, a tube station are all jammed together in an absurdly narrow winding street, which topographically has remained a country lane. It is ever busy and overcrowded, but the funny part is that its merrily bustling crowd bears the stamp of middle age and eminent respectability. Nowhere (except at the Royal Academy) can one see such remarkable hats and so many comfortably off old ladies. No Society smartness here, but "upper- and middle-class" writ large; and that is its charm, for this is a section of London's population one does not see much elsewhere. High Street, matinées, the Royal Academy, tea in Kensington Gardens, moderate High Church, and "genuine white sales," seem to me to belong together. It is all very Victorian, very reassuring, and slightly comic.

If all these streets are essentially feminine shopping centres, men have their own in St. James's, which is not confined to St. James's Street only, which we have already described; for there is SAVILE ROW, with SACK-VILLE STREET running it close, which are to masculine clothes what the Rue de la Paix is to feminine. Both are full of pleasant and simple eighteenth-century houses, almost each of which contains a tailor's shop which most carefully not only exhibits nothing whatsoever in its window but obscures it with wire-netting or some other non-transparent contrivance to exclude the gaze

58 JANUARY SALES: Contemplation

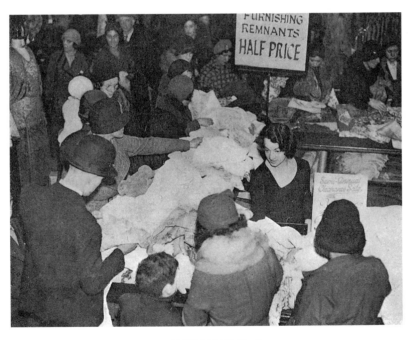

59 JANUARY SALES: Realisation

60 THE SECRETARY OF STATE'S ROOM, THE FOREIGN OFFICE

61 THE STONE CLIFFS OF WHITEHALL: The Horse Guards, the
War Office, and the Foreign Office

of the profane. Then there are the two ARCADES off
Piccadilly, with their, dazzling vision of ties, shirts,
socks, scarves, and pullovers, which I quite seriously
consider the best proof of an innate British sense of
colour; for only artists can invent such colour schemes.
These are the streets sacred to bachelor's flats and
lodgings and Turkish Baths, and discreet hotels, such
as JERMYN STREET, which retains a slight flavour of
Regency dissipation.

If the more, frivolous and more social part of the
masculine domain is St. James's, its more serious and
political headquarters are in Whitehall. WHITEHALL is
the "High Street" of the British Empire, and as such is
without parallel. Following London's tradition of concentration, all that is essential to the ruling of the nation
is represented there in one spot; but it is equally characteristic that this system is not rigidly adhered to. Whitehall was as little planned for its purpose as the British
Empire—it just gradually grew to be what it is now,
on the site of Whitehall Palace, of which the Banqueting
Hall alone remains. Whitehall begins in cramped confusion in Trafalgar Square; some shops, a very new
theatre, a big bank, after which it gradually widens and
becomes Imperial. There stand the old classical Admiralty
and the more fanciful "Horse Guards," with its living
centaur statuary; and all the "Offices" (much too humble
a term) follow on both sides: War Office, Home Office,
Foreign, Colonial, and India Offices, etc., amidst which
rises the Cenotaph with its flags and wreaths, while a
plain old house in narrow Downing Street houses the
Prime Minister.

Now at last Whitehall opens out wide to the astonishingly contrasting vision of Gothic Westminster. Whitehall is white and black, pillared and Renascence;
Westminster is a grey, golden brown, and mediaeval—
a surprisingly picturesque medley of ancient and modern
with its thirteenth-century Hall, Abbey of many ages,
flanked by St. Margaret's, seeming to sail alongside the
larger vessel, and the Victorian—Gothic towers of the
Houses of Parliament.

Where Westminster faces the Thames begins the
EMBANKMENT, and reminds one of how extraordinarily
forgotten and neglected is London's great river. The
Seine is a central artery of Paris, its quays full of life, and
magnificent buildings for miles on end; in London the
Thames is a frontier behind which begins the unknown
and neglected. The Embankment is one of the few and
comparatively short stretches of quays along the river,
and no one seems to have cared much what buildings
grew up along what should have been London's grandest
road. After the very ugly Scotland Yard you pass Whitehall Court, which at any rate has size, the charming
Adelphi, dwarfed by the Savoy Hotel and the white
Shell Building, with its great clock, and arrive at the
spot where, with the fine façade of Somerset House and
St. Paul's cupola swimming in the sky, the Embankment
is what it should be. But it does not remain so long,
but breaks out into modern red-brick Tudor, and ends
—after passing the green Temple Garden—for no
particular reason, in a curve, at Blackfriars Bridge. On
the other side of the river there is the County Hall,
dignified if uninspired, and there are wharves, chimneys,
factories—things called ugly, but beautified by mist,
clouds, or sun. Yet it is a pity that they did not construct
the Embankment on that side, for from there alone can
you see an ensemble, a picture of London which remains
impressed on the mind as truly representative. As things
are you can only see it from the end of Waterloo
Bridge or London Bridge, those true entrance-gates of
the City.

The Embankment hides London's Historical water-
front, the STRAND, which is doubtless its most famous
street. Its character has, of course, entirely changed,
for in old times it ran at the back of palaces built on
the river, of which only Somerset House, now set back
from the water, remains. Otherwise there are but names:
Savoy, Northumberland, etc., and a single water-gate,
and the little Savoy Chapel. A very beautiful London
has vanished here for ever, and one which knew that
its river might rival the Venetian Grand Canal. Ever

since then the Strand has continued to change its aspect, and is doing so at present, for in the last twenty years both this and its character have changed entirely. A generation ago it was still the centre of London's theatre and night life, its "Boulevard," but now all that life has moved farther west. Instead, the Strand is becoming an "Empire" street. The Dominions have built their houses here, Canada and South Africa in Trafalgar Square, Australia and New Zealand in the Strand, India just behind it; the Strand is London's great Dominions Street. It stands for "dear old London" to the exiles, who have brought their tropical outfits in its shops, even if there is little left that can be called old. It is one of the most alive streets of London, not quite the City yet, but leading up to it. It is a men's street, a City-rush street, also a tourists' street. One has a feeling that the people one passes have just come back from Rhodesia, or are just off to India; and it is always full of men who look a little lost, as if they did not quite know their way about.

The Strand begins in Trafalgar Square, called by its detractors the most wasted space in Europe, which is a gross exaggeration. The National Gallery is not bad, though they might remove that silly little cupola and the other roof excrescences, and St. Martin's is one of London's very best churches. But the central asphalt desert of the square is really very depressing, and only on Sundays do the pigeons and the orators make it more tolerable. Charing Cross looks what it is—doomed; the glories of Continental traffic are lost to its station; and its hotel attracts people for its quiet (a world-famous musician always stays there for that reason). Opposite, the last old houses have gone; next to it are grimy houses with cheap shops, bound to disappear before long—it is not a very promising beginning for an "Imperial Highway." But after that matters improve; the twentieth-century Strand begins with the New Adelphi buildings, hiding the old, the new Tivoli, the new (very new) Adelphi Theatre, the new Strand Palace, etc. But the Strand's great glory is its perspective, for

what other street in the world has two churches standing
behind each other in the middle of the road? Both are
delightful, but the first is my favourite, and it has even
managed to retain its charm in spite of the colossal (and
very effective) Bush House. Bush House, with ALDWYCH
and KINGSWAY behind it, are newest London, very large
and very white, good in general-effect if not in detail.
Facing them stands Somerset House, with its grand
deserted courtyard, and then the Strand ends in a jumble
of the graceful spire of St. Clement's, the pseudo-Gothic
Law Courts and ponderous Australia House; passes what
was Temple Bar, and enters the City as FLEET STREET.
Here the Law and the Press hold sway. Fleet Street
traverses a maze full of hidden surprises. The Temple
and Lincoln's Inn and Dr. Johnson's house and the Old
Cheshire Cheese and St. Bride's, with the most astonishing of Wren's steeples, are but a few of them. The
street itself has a few old houses, St. Dunstan's rebuilt
but charming, and for the rest newspapers in old or newer
or brand-new buildings, such as that of the *Daily Tele-
graph* and the black glass modernist *Daily Express*. The
papers of all the English-speaking world have their
offices here and in the streets, alleys, courts, and passages
all around it; it is the acropolis of the printing-press. It
manages to look mediaeval, though nearly all its houses
are new, and it ends in a burst of glory with the finest
view of St. Paul's rising on Ludgate Hill.

It would be easy to write several volumes about
the streets of London without exhausting the subject, but it
is a more difficult task to choose those of the greatest
interest. Where is London most interesting? PARK LANE
is curious enough. It looks like the Brighton Parade
facing a park instead of the sea, and it is London's
Avenue du Bois or Tiergartenstrasse, associated with
millions made in South Africa and odd sham-Tudor
palaces of the nineteenth century. Now the biggest
new houses of London are arising here, huge hotels,
flats, clubs. Some of the private mansions survive,
but Park Lane is doomed to share the fate of all

62   THE CHANGING RIVER FRONT: The Last of Waterloo Bridge, with the new Buildings on the Victoria Embankment

63   NEWSPAPER FACTORY IN FLEET STREET

Mayfair. Flats and hotels are the headquarters of the rich of to-day, and here a new centre is arising for their benefit. It is bright and new and expensive-looking, and represents the post-war spirit with its defects and its advantages. It is interesting because it is quite of the present, and there is so much that is old left in London that it can well afford an outburst of modernity. But is this cocktail London as interesting as that of the CALEDONIAN MARKET, where once a week you can see the most stupendous *Foire* in the world, with which neither those of Paris, Rome, or Madrid can compare? Here are acres of every imaginable sort of second-hand objects for sale, from broken plates to costly Chinese porcelain, from discarded stoves to Queen Anne silver, from dirty old mattresses to Chippendale chairs. You may buy old clothes or stuffed birds or a Royal coat of arms or a Siamese Buddha with an enigmatic smile. Food there is as well, and there are miles of new cotton or wool-stuffs, and thousands of housewives with news-paper parcels and nets and perambulators, and curio-dealers or amateurs bargain-hunting. Indians in turbans are selling peanuts, children run wild, and generally a fresh breeze is blowing over this northern hill. This is the busy, popular, cheery workmen's London, with plenty to occupy eye and brain. Or should one prefer other markets? WHITECHAPEL with its dense crowd packed into narrow alleys and the biggest noise in Britain: screaming salesmen, loud-speakers, gramo-phones, old Jews with side-curls and young ones in gaudy scarves, ready to conquer the Western world. Nor are there Jews only. Hindus are selling scarves; there are Red Indians and negroes—real negroes from Africa; and there are all sorts of jugglers, acrobats, musicians, and vendors of patent medicines. It is a fair beside a market, and though it is as exotic as the Caledonian is British, yet it could only be found in London. Or else you may prefer COVENT GARDEN in the early morning, with its mountains of fruit and vegetables and flowers, its huge carthorses, guarded by the Opera House and a church, a vegetable pande-

monium amongst the remnants of what was the grandest
and most Italianate residential square of seventeenth-
century London. But there are many other lesser markets,
quite as entertaining in their way: BREWER STREET, with
its mixture of Belgian French, Jewish, and English
stalls and shops, or SHEPHERD'S BUSH ARCHES, so
noisily cheerful, hiding one of the best shops for Chinese
art treasures among its cheap modern goods, and where
you may acquire a canary for sixpence and carry it off
in a paper bag if you win in the lottery. Or if one wishes
for quiet meditation, one might look at HARLEY STREET,
where the doctors live, and all the wealthy in the land
must go for treatment. A doctor must live in Harley
Street, as a tailor must live in Savile Row, or a jeweller in
Bond Street; and this is a mystery, for must a doctor
pass an examination before he is allowed to reside there
and thereby becomes a prominent man, or does he auto-
matically become clever as soon as he moves there? Is
HATTON GARDEN, all diamonds, more extraordinary, or
SPITALFIELDS, with the last descendants of families which
have been silk-weavers for centuries; or that small East
End peninsula, discovered by a reporter not long ago
in dockland, where all the people descend from one
family and live and die in a tiny little world of their own?
It is quite certain that no one will ever know all London's
streets of interest, but there is one thing I am far less
certain about, and that is whether the most interesting
streets are not those thousands and thousands of no
fame and no character, where unobtrusive little brick
or stucco houses follow each other mile after mile, and
where the great anonymous masses live. For they seem
to me to hold the key to the secret soul of London one
will never know, as one will never discover what are the
lives of the millions of men and women, all dissimilar,
hidden behind their Nottingham-lace curtains; for
London is most fantastic where it is least picturesque,
remarkable, or famous.

64   THE CALEDONIAN MARKET, ISLINGTON

65   HYDE PARK: Winter in Rotten Row

CHAPTER IV

GREEN LONDON

At heart the English are not really townfolk like the Latins, but country lovers, and what they like best in their cities are their parks and gardens and trees. The art of gardening has a very old tradition in England, influenced by Italy, France, and Holland, until it found its own character in the eighteenth century and influenced the Continent in its turn. Briefly, English landscape gardening refuses to violate nature by imposing geometrical designs upon it, but tries to retain its character while correcting and improving it. Thus London arrives at very different results from Paris. The French *jardin*, even on the scale of Versailles, continues the architecture of the house or palace, and forms one whole with it; the English idea is to preserve a piece of country and fit a house into it, or even hide a house in it. The London parks are, as far as this can be achieved, pieces of country left in the midst of town, but this can be achieved only because the English country is already park-like. This is their first, but by no means their only striking characteristic, for London's parks are for use, and the Londoners unrivalled in the art of using a park. Compare the Tuileries and Champs-Élysées with Hyde Park, which occupies a corresponding site; Paris created the world's finest street perspective and laid out beautiful gardens, but all you can do in them is to walk or to sit, and not for one minute will you forget that you are in town. Hyde Park, enclosed by railings, is a separate world; at its gates town ceases; cars go round it, inside is peace. Hyde Park is not, I consider, London's loveliest park, but it is its most many-sided. There is Rotten Row for riders and the morning Church Parade (which has lost a good deal of its glory) for Sundays, and this part of the park is full of flower-beds. It is a garden, but a garden where you walk or sit on the lawns. There is a bandstand, and there is really good music to be heard

L

close by; there is the Serpentine for boating and bathing
(though "the Lido" is rather grand a name for its bathing
facilities). There is the famous space near Marble Arch
where meetings are held and all and sundry may speak
if they can find an audience, but best of all there are huge
expanses of lawn with groups of trees, where Londoners
lie ot sit about and laze, and there is enough open space
for fresh air to pass over them. London does not—
except in the East End—walk in its streets for pleasure;
when the Londoner has time he goes for a walk in the park, the
next best thing to going to the country, and
looks at the sheep grazing. He can picnic there, and need
not go to distant woods for that. The park is for all
classes, but nothing is more remarkable and charming
to observe than the manner in which they respect each
other's codes. There is nothing to prevent the most
ragged from lying on the grass where the chairs of
fashion stand, but he does not intrude any more than
fashion would dream of spoiling happy family parties by
supercilious looks. Hyde Park on summer Sundays shows
all London of all classes sharing its gifts in amity.

KENSINGTON GARDENS adjoins Hyde Park, so that they really
form one whole, yet it is different both in aspect
and in public. Kensington Gardens is an eighteenth-
century creation, laid out in straight avenues (of which
the Broad Walk is the finest), like Versailles, for of
course the gardens belong to the Palace. But English
taste has modified their geometrical conception, and the
trees are left to assume the shapes that please them and
the avenues are not of gravel but of turf. The Gardens
are full of charming surprises. There is the flower-walk
with its masses of colour, and the Sunk Garden near the
Palace, which is a little gem and as complete in itself as
a Persian garden, and the Paved Garden and fountain,
overlooking the lake. There are hills and slopes, and
there is the Round Pond, which is not round, where
children sail a miniature fleet. The Gardens are a children's paradise, and so it is fitting that Peter Pan should
have his statue there, though I think it anything but an
admirable work of art. Nor would I miss Watts's statue

66, 67   HYDE PARK: Winter and Summer by the Serpentine

68   UNEMPLOYMENT IN HYDE PARK

69   EMPLOYMENT IN COVENT GARDEN

of "Physical Energy," which looks lop-sided from all sides and does not improve the wide vista across the Gardens. But then it is a children's park, and I am sure they don't mind in the least and are not interested in the quarrels of those who prefer Peter Pan and the others who prefer Epstein's "Rima." Nor do the trim nurses or mothers who push the prams. Kensington Gardens is not controversial in spirit; it is a domain of a well-fed bourgeoisie, not smart but decorous. Even the Palace is not palatial, but homely, bourgeois, Dutch. Old ladies live in the Palace, and other old ladies drink their tea in the tea pavilion, and there is a statue of Queen Victoria by one of her relations which fittingly presides, and which is very much pleasanter than the official "Memorial."

An inhabitant of Kensington could walk quite a number of miles, right to the centre of London, Trafalgar Square, without ever leaving parks, except to cross at Hyde Park Corner. London is unique in the possession of these stretches of green in its midst. He would leave Hyde Park through a marble gate and enter the Green Park through a triumphal arch, and it might strike him that London has little sense of the formally majestic, and does not quite know what to do with its "triumphal arches." That may be because triumphal arches do not go well with a sense of humour. This triumphal arch is surmounted by the work of an army officer, so I expect its horses are quite correct, but its proportion to the arch is not. The arch contains no relics of victory, but a police-post, just as that other arch opening on Trafalgar Square contains offices, and so they are perhaps useful; but really nothing more can be said for Marble Arch in its present position. There it stands, forlorn on an island with the traffic-stream around it, and opens upon nothing whatsoever, triumphant or otherwise. Our present arch, however, leads to the GREEN PARK, most fittingly named, for it is little else but green. It is more purely natural than any other of the centrally situated parks; there are just hillocks and trees and grass and space. It is always full of men lying prone on the grass, and dogs and children, and it has fine wide prospects to the tower of Westminster Cathedral, and a monumental gate of wrought iron, removed from old Devonshire House, which is kept most annoyingly closed, while you have to squeeze in through narrow openings next to it. The Green Park is no more than a "lung," and an introduction to St. James's Park, but ST. JAMES'S PARK is the most fascinating of all parks. It is different in character from the others, for its charm is not rural and does not lie in space and freedom and a sense of escape from town, but on the contrary in the buildings and monuments which surround it. It is their beauty and still more the associations they evoke which make St. James's Park unique. To a man gifted with a little imagination, it appears as the centre of the British Empire and of British history. Its most perfect spot is the narrow bridge over the lake, for there you will find the loveliest view in all London, and, if you use the mind as well as the eye, the widest prospect of history. You see Buckingham Palace with the Royal Standard flying above it, the Memorial before it, to remind you of Victoria, and the Mall to remind you of her son, King Edward. There is the London Museum, and St. James's Palace with memories of levées and conferences; there is Marlborough House where the beautiful Alexandra ended her days, and Carlton House Terrace with the York Column; while the Nelson Column.is seen in the distance. To the west arises a fantastic white city of cupolas and roofs and turrets, which on closer inspection reveals the Horse Guards and War Office, the Italian palace of the Foreign Office, hiding Downing Street and the India Office. Next come the spires and towers of Westminster, of Abbey and Parliament, the houses of Queen Anne's Gate, the beauty of which cannot be seen from here, and the black pile of Queen Anne's Mansions, all too visible, with the white tower of the Underground, full of luminous beauty at night, and the classical barracks—where you can see the strange rites accompanying the changing of guards—brings you back once more to

70, 71   KENSINGTON GARDENS: The Great Avenue and the Serpentine

72, 73   THE HOUSEHOLD TROOPS—On Duty and Off

74   KENSINGTON GARDENS: Winter on the Round Pond

75　ST JAMES'S PARK: Looking across the Lake to Whitehall

Buckingham Palace. The ghosts of history are all round you: Elizabeth and Mary, whom she had executed, sleep close to each other in the Abbey, with ever so many other kings and queens. From Edward the Confessor to King Edward VII stretches the perspective. There are the memories of Charles, beheaded over there in Whitehall, and of the Parliament which ordered his execution; there are memories of all the wars down to the last. Some rulers are beheaded and others get grand memorials, and others—like Queen Anne—funny little statues tucked away in a corner, and some generals get a grand column, though no one remembers what for, and others, well remembered, get none at all.

And so the centuries pass, and the Gothic spires and classical pillars and the Tudor brick and the Regency stucco and the grimy nineteenth century and the very white twentieth all combine to be the present and to-day. And if you are tired of stone and history, there are the perfect trees and the flower-beds, the green velvet of the lawn, the many-coloured waterfowl, and the scream-ing, fluttering, white gulls. And so St. James's Park is not only one of the most perfect places in London, but one of the great sights of the world.

Next to St. James's I would place REGENT'S PARK in beauty. It forms part of Nash's great architectural scheme, and is surrounded by his light and monumental terraces. I believe this is the only park in the world placed in the midst of a definite architectural scheme; it is certainly the only one I have ever come across, and park and buildings form an ensemble of very great dis-tinction. The park itself is very diverse, and it has the finest "scenery" in London round its lake, with its willows and swans and canoes, and its delicious children's pond. It has vast expanses, and geometrical flower-beds and vases near its great avenue, where the squirrels come and make friends with one, and it is so large that it hides Botanical Gardens and a College and St. Dunstan's Lodge, and the enormous Zoo. The Zoo is one of the most important of its kind, and I find it as depressing as all such institutions, for I fail to see that a prison for animals is more cheerful than one for human beings. Regent's Park is very beautiful indeed, but fashion tends to despise it nevertheless. Fashionable London has not followed Nash's invitation, and neglects the perfect houses he built for it; it went west, but refused to go north. Quite poor people live behind the grand façades of some of the more easterly terraces, in Somerstown and Camden Town, nor is there often vast wealth to be found in the west, and it is moderate north of the park. So the people among the flowers and swans and squirrels are not elegant, but the boys playing cricket on the fields and the innumerable children do not seem to mind much. And it seems to me that all the eccentrics of London foregather in Regent's Park.

There is one more centrally situated park in London, though people think it out of the way, because it lies on the southern bank of the Thames—BATTERSEA PARK. This is a typical English park of the nineteenth century, with trees and lawns, cricket and football grounds, but its great charm is its river terrace. It is distinctly a poor people's park, but poor people being much more sensible than rich you will find them in all the innumerable green oases of London. For these are indeed innumerable, and that is one of London's best features. VICTORIA PARK is a huge playground for the north-eastern districts, but the favourite place of the masses is HAMPSTEAD HEATH. That northern hill-district is indeed extraordinary. Hampstead Hill is not unlike Montmartre in position, but it has remained a large open space, really a heath with ponds and pines and wide views. Hampstead village still has old wooden houses and many eighteenth-century villas, and Hampstead Heath is continued by KEN WOOD, with its Adam mansion, containing a picture gallery. The Spaniards Road with its old inns connects it with the neighbouring hill of HIGHGATE, with another park and more old houses, whence more roads flanked by woods lead to ALEXANDRA PALACE and the gardens on Muswell Hill. These northern hills are a characteristic jumble of woods and heath and parks and built-over spaces; it may seem purely

76   KENSINGTON PALACE

77   BUCKINGHAM PALACE

78   A LANDMARK IN THE ARCHITECTURE: The Crystal Palace, Sydenham, from the Air

accidental to find large tracts of country left intact, but it is really most admirable to find them preserved for ever, for London has long grown beyond them, and they are, of course, extremely valuable building-sites. On a smaller scale PRIMROSE HILL, north of Regent's Park, is just such a preserve, no more than one of the hundreds of small hills of London, but one that has not been built over. It is a charming and unexpected bit of country with a wide view over the trees of the park to distant St. Paul's. It is just such unexpected spots which make London so delightful, for what other city was ever content to let a green hill in its midst just remain a green hill without "improving" it?

The south has its hills like the north, and on one of them stands the CRYSTAL PALACE, with its fine grounds, which has lived long enough to be admired again as "the first modern building" by the most radically modern architects, after having been called absurd, old-fashioned, and early Victorian by the preceding generation. To the south also belongs GREENWICH PARK, perhaps laid out by Lenotre, but much anglicised. Of all London's surprises, Greenwich is perhaps the greatest. After an endless ride through mean and poor quarters you see a fine Baroque church, and suddenly, round a corner, lies Greenwich Palace, one of the grandest Baroque palaces of Europe. It was meant to be approached from the river, whence you step up to the terrace between the four great pavilions with their cupolas, to which Lenotre's hill-park forms a background. Now it is crowned by the Observatory (where all time comes from), and you can walk on the meridian and thus be neither east nor west of it, and then continue your walk for miles on Blackheath behind the hill. In front of the palace there is a little quay, and there are some quaint old inns, while steamers and barges are for ever passing along the waterway before you, and it is all as odd as if you had stumbled across a *Sans Souci* in the east end of Berlin.

The royal palaces west of London are not thus hidden from sight. It is curious how London likes to form

"chains" of parks or gardens: Kensington Gardens—
Hyde Park—the Green Park—St. James's Park is such
a chain; Hampstead—Ken Wood—Highgate—Muswell
Hill another, and on the Thames there is the chain of
Kew—Richmond—Hampton Court—Bushy Park. KEW
GARDENS, the nearest, are, I think, the most perfect
gardens in the world, for it takes a damp climate to
produce perfection in vegetation, and here each tree or
plant is a perfect specimen of its kind. For Kew Gardens
are one of the greatest Botanical Gardens of the world.
Thank God they do not look in the least scientific! I have
never visited the greatest Herbarium in the world, which
is there, and the hot-houses and palm-houses look to
me exactly like all the others I have seen; but nowhere
are there such marvellous trees (the names of which
I ignore), each a royal personage, nor delights like the
iris-gardens and ponds, the rose-clusters overhanging
a basin, the all-blue garden, the azaleas, the absurd little
classical temples bequeathed by the eighteenth century,
the Pagoda—that towering *chinoiserie*—and, best of all,
the Rhododendron Walk. Here, in June, you may see
the most gorgeous colour feast a garden can provide,
and the path and the valley through which it winds are
so cunningly devised that all is excluded from view
except those multi-coloured masses of bloom. Kew
Gardens are really one of the much talked of and seldom
met with blessings of democracy!

RICHMOND has its lovely and world-famous terrace,
and its park which is not a park, but a grand stretch of
open country with hills and copses, deer and squirrels
and birds, sturdy oaks and beeches, where one may well
lose oneself. HAMPTON COURT, on the other hand, has
the most formal of all London's palace gardens.
William III wanted to make Hampton Court his Versailles, but fortunately failed, for there are quite enough
second-rate imitations of that unique place about. The
beautiful Tudor buildings with their deep red brick and
fantastic chimneys were left intact, and Wren's classical
façade faces the other way. There are plenty of treasures
in the Palace, including the ghost of Catherine Howard,

the Great Hall, with its fine roof and tapestries, and the picture-galleries, and the formal gardens contain most beautiful informal flower-borders. The "chain" comes to an end with BUSHY PARK, the chief glory of which is its grand avenues of chestnuts, rivalling that of the Vienna PRATER.

To these "royal parks" must be added the "Commons," large stretches of land, part park part purely heath, of which the most beautiful is that of WIMBLEDON continued by Putney Heath. But you will find the map of Greater London dotted with such green patches: heaths, commons, and greens, while inner London contains a huge number of smaller green spaces, whose very smallness in that sea of brick and stone gives them a pathetic charm of their own. There are a number of them all along the river: FULHAM with its episcopal palace; CHELSEA with Cheyne Walk and the Hospital Gardens; the gardens adjoining WESTMINSTER PALACE and facing those of LAMBETH PALACE; the long, narrow stretch of the EMBANKMENT GARDENS, with their tea and concerts for tired City clerks and typists; the TOWER GARDENS with its terrace and guns—down to Greenwich. Then you will find plenty around the old churches, for London loves to leave them surrounded by a patch of churchyard and trees. You will find them around ST. JOHN'S of St. John's Wood, ST. JAMES'S of Piccadilly, ST. ANNE'S of Soho, behind the Oratory, behind Mecklenburgh Square (where at present the Foundling Hospital site is till a playground); and you will find many diminutive green yards around the City churches. And then there are the SQUARES, most English of English inventions! A real London square (for there are some wrongly thus designated) is a truly British compromise, for its gardens are neither public nor quite private. In more truly democratic countries they would, of course, be public, only the trouble is that these more truly democratic countries don't cover the centres of their squares with lawns and trees, but as a rule with concrete pavement; so that there the garden squares are public but very few, while in London they belong to the residents

M

only, and are innumerable. They are, indeed, one of
London's greatest attractions, but they are not by any
means evenly distributed over its surface. To my mind,
the most perfect squares are those of BLOOMSBURY,
which is so rich in them that they almost touch each
other. Each has its garden and none of them are quite
alike, but it is the combination of the central gardens
and the surrounding architecture which make up the
character of a London square, and Bloomsbury has
about the best domestic architecture in London. Its
largest is RUSSELL SQUARE, which has the best garden,
full of lilac and laburnum in spring, but has lost its architectural unity. Its west side has some good old houses,
but on the eastern stand some of London's greatest
eyesores. BEDFORD SQUARE is the perfect square with
lovely gardens and perhaps the finest houses in London,
all but a few given over to societies, consulates, or
publishers. The few private owners, like Lady Oxford,
deserve congratulation. Next in architectural perfection
come MECKLENBURGH SQUARE, with its mixture of
brick and stucco, and BRUNSWICK SQUARE, but I would
not care to offend any of the others, not GORDON
SQUARE with its modern but good Gothic church and
impressive intellectuals, nor TAVISTOCK SQUARE, very
perfect in building, nor even TORRINGTON SQUARE,
though it is too long and full of cheap boarding-houses,
nor QUEEN'S SQUARE and BLOOMSBURY SQUARE, though
they have fallen from grace and allowed many old houses
to be replaced by horrors. There are some very pleasant
squares beyond the boundaries of Bloomsbury as well,
such as REGENT SQUARE, with a miniature York Cathedral and a pillared Regency church and stunted trees, and
the odd little PERCY CIRCUS sloping down from a surprisingly
steep little hill; RED LION SQUARE to the north
of Bloomsbury with a medley of old and very new, and,
to the west of it, FITZROY SQUARE, where Adam built
some of his finest façades and where there are some of
London's finest trees.

It is the fate of Central London's squares to "march
with the times," which means that they are in a state of

79   HAMPTON COURT: Wren's Garden Front, with the Tudor Towers and Chimneys behind

80   SUNDAY PROCESSION ON THE EMBANKMENT

permanent transition. Of such is SOHO SQUARE, where beautiful old houses, modern offices, hospitals, and a church try to get on with each other; GOLDEN SQUARE, growing up all around spasmodically; HANOVER SQUARE, following this bad example more slowly, while retaining fine gardens; and its neighbour CAVENDISH SQUARE, which still has many beautiful residences. Most of these squares, incidentally, contain statues, often very good and always quite unnoticed. The largest central square, and in fact the largest of any of London's squares, LINCOLN'S INN FIELDS, is not a "proper square" at all, for its gardens are public. It has the most magnificent plane-trees in London, and it is very beautiful, but it is so large that it no longer manages to impress one as a single whole. The buildings do not combine to form one picture with the gardens, but many are beautiful taken singly. There is the Inn itself, Newcastle House, one of the grandest residences of Stuart times, and Lindsey House near it, the Law Society buildings, and the building of the Auctioneers' Institute, new but satisfactory. In the gardens you may see people playing croquet (is it played anywhere else nowadays?) and a rather charming monument to Margaret MacDonald with many bronze children on it and many real children on its stone bench. Another square with public if small gardens is LEICESTER SQUARE, where an incongrous Shakespeare monument stands between the cinemas and the traffic's roar, and where passers-by may rest for a short moment to feed the pigeons.

But real squares must be residential, and their home is the West End. Some are famous, most known only to the people living near them. Berkeley Square and Grosvenor Square are famous indeed, and all the heroes and heroines of really high-class novels live there. BERKELEY SQUARE is fast becoming commercialised, but it can still be proud of its gardens, and so can GROSVENOR SQUARE, which is a very fine expanse, though I think its houses heavy and gloomy compared to those of Bloomsbury. ST. JAMES'S SQUARE again will always remain attractive, though it is difficult to say why, for there

are many indifferent modern houses there, and some
of the historical ones, like Norfolk House with its low
windows, are not particularly beautiful either. But the
most noble of West End squares are not among the
most famous. One of these is REGENT'S PARK SQUARE
with its beautiful curve, unity of architectural design,
and that air of subdued grandeur proper to all that
survives of Nash's great scheme, linking Carlton House
with the terraces of Regent's Park. BELGRAVE SQUARE
is the most impressive residential square; less perfect in
detail than Nash's work, it yet retains great dignity, and
its octagonal shape, due to the four large independent
mansions at the corners, is unique in London. CHESTER
SQUARE and EATON SQUARE almost rival it, though their
extreme length inclines to give them the character of
streets.

If these squares impress by their unity of style and
their size, SMITH SQUARE in Westminster owes its
charm to the very opposite. It is small, and so are its
eighteenth-century houses which might almost be called
cottages, but they are very perfect of their kind. Behind
them the Victoria Tower appears huge and square;
intermixed with the old buildings are modern ones,
more or less successfully imitating their style, while the
centre of the square is taken up by what is surely the
weirdest Baroque church in England. CADOGAN GARDENS
is right to insist on its garden aspect, for its long stretches
are very lovely, while the houses around are of all sorts
and ages. That strange and somewhat shabby-genteel
district, PIMLICO, has many pleasant Early Victorian
squares, and one huge open square, VINCENT SQUARE,
near which stands one of the best new buildings of
London, that of the Horticultural Society. All the West
End south and north of Hyde Park and Kensington
Gardens is full of Victorian residential squares, and
they are all pleasant if not particularly distinguished.
They have light stucco houses and those pillared porticoes
(there must be more columns in London than in the
rest of the universe put together) which the architects
of that time seem to have thought indispensable, and

the only possible porch. These are roomy, solidly comfortable, decent, and unimaginative houses, and the
squares represent the best solution of the problem of
how to live in the central part of a metropolis while
retaining quiet, green surroundings and comparatively
good air, that I have found anywhere. SOUTH KENSING-
TON, BAYSWATER, PADDINGTON, WESTBOURNE PARK
are so full of these that their character is determined by
them. Still farther west there are some charming old
squares to be found. Kensington has KENSINGTON
SQUARE, which retains some good Queen Anne houses,
while the small houses of EDWARDES SQUARE date from
the Regency; and charming, too, are some of the squares
of Chelsea, like TRAFALGAR SQUARE and ROYAL AVENUE.

CHAPTER V

LONDON AND THE ARTS

No useful purpose is served by comparisons of the artistic merit of different capitals, but surely London rivals any other city as a treasure-house of art, and it is rather strange to see so many sons and daughters of Albion religiously wending their way through the galleries of Florence or Rome, or the Louvre, and giving so little thought to their own. The artistic wealth of London is incalculable, and its galleries and museums are admirable. There are two kinds of museums in the world, I find: the admirable and the lovable; and London's greatest collections belong to the former variety. The BRITISH MUSEUM is magnificent and severe. Its strictly classical façade (spoilt by some of those railings which are the curse of London) indicates its spirit, and its austere halls and galleries are full of unique treasures. A place like the Museum or like the Louvre may be a source of endless pleasure or become a nightmare. To an unfortunate tourist who feels he must "do" it it appears as a nightmarish confusion; if you want to derive pleasure from it you must go and call on only a few "friends" at a time, and everyone's choice of friends will be different. Everyone will, I suppose, go to the Elgin marbles, but some may prefer the Nimrod room or the Lion-hunt, or Egypt. You may marvel at the perfection of the early English miniatures (and wonder what happened to painting in England from the fifteenth to the eighteenth century), or you may prefer those of Persia. The china collection is a marvel, but so are the gold ornaments, and it is for you to choose which you want to see. You can wonder at the strange imaginings of "native" art or turn your back on the savages and try to solve the highly sophisticated smile of the Buddha images. Visit that Etruscan tomb, so oddly modern, or the priceless collection of prints; cast a fleeting glance at library and reading-room or spend your life there. Do whatever

81   ROYAL ACADEMY PRIVATE VIEW

82   LUNCH-TIME LECTURE AT THE NATIONAL GALLERY

83   ART SALES: The Caledonian Market

84   ART SALES: Christie's Auction Rooms

you like except one thing: don't try to "see the British Museum."

The NATIONAL GALLERY is quite as admirable in its way, and it may seem a simpler proposition as it limits itself to pictures. But this, again, is deceptive, for if you are going to enjoy yourself you must not mix Holbein and Titian, Rembrandt and Claude Lorrain, for such mixtures are indigestible and the cocktail idea is inappropriate in art. Here, again, you must choose and choose well, for the most famous works are not necessarily the most interesting or lovely. I don't think Uccello's cavalry battle is counted amongst them, but it is one of the great treasures of the gallery all the same. The Florentines are wonderful (incidentally all the pictures are kept in admirable condition), but I prefer Botticelli's unique "Mars and Venus" to his all too frequent and similar versions of "The Virgin with the Infant Jesus," to which I prefer Duccio's Madonna and some other Sienese pictures. Titian is magnificently represented, but Moroni is here superior to Tintoretto. There may, however, be days when all Italian art seems wearisome and too much in the grand manner, and when the intimate, simple, and everyday Dutch art suits one's mood better. Well, there is Peter de Hooch and there is Hobbema, and of course there is Rembrandt—but he is for tragic moods. Some days are Holbein days when nothing satisfies except the cool, objective, matter-of-fact perfection of his "Duchess of Milan," and on others the sombre black of the Spaniards will be the right thing for you. But one should never forget, I think, that this is, after all, the British National Gallery, for English pictures you will hardly find out of England. Their appreciation in the outer world is of a curiously mixed kind, for while they are now generally valued none too high by leading writers and critics (all eighteenth-century art being at a discount) they command formidable prices in the sale-rooms—but then at the doors of sale-rooms begins mystery to the profane. At any rate Reynolds has a beautiful golden tone of his own and Gainsborough has his grace and freshness (though I think his famous

"Mrs. Siddons" quite hideous with the crude red of the curtain and the disagreeably striped dress), but probably Raeburn should be put before either. Hogarth is a very great man indeed, and his "Shrimp Girl" is here, and impudently alive; Constable is most important in European painting, and Turner is a genius, if an incomplete one. But if you wish to get to know all these you must leave the National Gallery for its more modern sister, the Tate Gallery. The Tate Gallery is its necessary continuation, but to some extent they overlap. All Turner's later work and his water-colours are at the Tate, and to me they are the most extraordinary part of his work, but his most famous pictures remain at the National Gallery.

Some of the best work of the English eighteenth-century painters are here, some there (Hogarth's "Marriage a la Mode," for instance, is shown at the Tate), and the same applies to the work of Constable and Crome. The Tate Gallery will produce a mixed impression on visitors as all collections of modern pictures must, for they include much work which at present seems merely out of date and old-fashioned, a state all things have to pass through before being promoted to the dignity of the "antique" or the "historical." So at the Tate you will find the work of genius: of Blake (which you can see here alone), of the Pre-Raphaelites, who have but few admirers at present, and of Watts, who was almost a genius but an extraordinarily bad painter; also that of many R.A.'s from Leighton down to recent days, which provoke an anything but reverential attitude of mind in the spectator. But against that you must set the surprise of finding a collection of French Impressionist and later paintings such as you will vainly seek in Paris, containing such masterpieces as Manet's "Eva Gonzalez," Seurat's "La Baignade," and Van Gogh's "Sunflowers." You may like Sargent's immortalisation of the Wertheimer family, in which case I beg to disagree, for I find all his work meretricious and cheap, if clever. But there are the works of Conder and Whistler, delightful if not imposing, and there are, among the works of the living, some of really outstanding merit by men like Augustus John, Wilson Steer, Orpen, Sickert; and the sculptor Frank Dobson—to mention but a few.

The VICTORIA AND ALBERT MUSEUM is certainly London's greatest treasure-house in size, and it is second to none in interest. The building is an unfortunate example of magnificence without taste, its modern parts and façade dating from that period about 1900 which produced similar "palaces" all the world over; but you will cease to think of it once inside its portals. The next impression, if you are new to it and if you ever hope to get to know its contents, will, however, be one of intense alarm at its size. Here are miles of art treasures on a number of floors, and as most of the exhibits are *objets d'art,* that are of small size, you may well despair. The variety is extraordinary, and this museum ought to be taken in very small doses only. It contains the art of all peoples and all times; there is Italian sculpture and there are the ivories, there are halls so large that façades of whole houses have been re-erected in them, and State barges swim on the floor. There are miles of furniture and of textiles (including the Syon cope, which is perhaps one of the greatest works of English art) and of ceramics, including the famous Salting Collection. There is lace and lacquer and silver and forged iron, and there are carpets and tapestries and costumes. And as if all these were not sufficiently bewildering, there are some collections housed here which are really separate museums, like the collection of Constable's landscapes, the Ionides Collection of the school of Fontainebleau, the Jones Collection of the French eighteenth century, and the Raphael cartoons for the tapestries in the Sistine Chapel! So you can spend months and years there without exhausting it, and your task will be facilitated by the fact that this museum is open till 9p.m. twice a week, which is a unique case as far as I know.

South Kensington is enough to drive any conscientious and hurried sightseeing tourist to suicide, for it is a

N

whole city of museums. Architecturally they are of varying merit, and some are very fine, but how magnificent an ensemble might have been formed here if there had been even a minor Wren or Nash to plan them all. As it is, each building is unrelated to the other, and they all hide each other. It seems to me that between them they contain all anybody in this world might possibly wish to see, and therefore any amount that one particular person (myself, for instance) is not interested in in the slightest. If you wish to see the skeletons of prehistoric animals, or minerals, or learn all about mining go to the NATURAL HISTORY MUSEUM (which looks like Tower Bridge), but if you prefer engines and aeroplanes and such things go to the SCIENCE MUSEUM instead. There is the IMPERIAL WAR MUSEUM for the bellicose, but the same building houses art needlework for the more peaceful; and there are galleries where all the products of the Empire are exhibited, and its most fascinating part has a museum all to itself—the INDIA MUSEUM. To a great extent, of course, all these museums are educational institutions; they are not places to wander about in in order to discover marvels, but citadels of instruction. They do not belong to the times when princes or cultivated men of less exalted station collected works of art or of "curiosity" because they loved them, but to a bourgeois and scientific age bent on acquiring learning, or "understanding" art and other things and on making them useful and productive. Which is, of course, why I call them admirable.

But others are lovable, because the men who made them loved their treasures, because they are human, being founded by persons instead of "bodies," and quite possibly, too, because they are not too large. London's most lovable gallery is the WALLACE COLLECTION, for it not only fulfils all these conditions, but the works of art are seen in their actual collector's house. There are very few collections of such a consistently high level. The armoury is magnificent, but the dominant note is that of French eighteenth-century art, and Paris holds no single collection equally representative. There is Watteau and Boucher and Fragonard ("The Swing"), and the very best furniture and bronze of that most sophisticatedly artistic period of European art, and the snuff-boxes and the miniatures. There is, besides, a great gallery which is worthy to rank beside the famous *Salon Carré*, for here are Rembrandt's "Centurion" and Rubens' "Rainbow" and Velasquez's "Portrait of a Lady with a Fan," and masterpieces of such great men as Reynolds and Poussin and Watteau, who appear almost as minor lights in that assembly. The Wallace Collection I class with the Cluny and the Carnavalet in Paris among the ideal museums of this world.

The SOANE MUSEUM is somewhat similar in character, though on a small scale. It is fascinating to see an average London house ingeniously transformed into a cabinet of curiosities. Here we have a cultured man of the early nineteenth century who was not one of the fabulously wealthy, collecting what was best in the art of his own time and combining it with that of all other periods or countries he admired. There is Hogarth's "Rake's Progress" series, and there are Reynolds and Turner amidst many Greek and Roman treasures, but there is an Egyptian sarcophagus as well in that basement catacomb. There is a Canaletto, but there are also remnants of Indian palace splendours and even Peruvian pottery, though that was only "discovered" by the twentieth century. Another very delightful collection is the LONDON MUSEUM, also lodged in a mansion, Stafford House, of about the same size as Hertford House, which contains the Wallace collection. Though it was only founded in 1911, it has an atmosphere all of its own, and an intimacy quite unofficial. It is a place for lovers of history to whom an object means more than a treatise or a lecture. The vest worn by Charles I on the scaffold, his watch and his handkerchief conjure up a far more vivid picture of that charming and unhappy monarch than all the books written about him. I do not find all those broken bits of pottery, found somewhere or other, particularly stimulating, but I like to see Queen Vic-

toria's dresses (what a tiny person she was!) and Queen
Alexandra's gorgeous robes (how lovely she must have
looked in them!). There are jewels and gold and sham
jewels and sham gold (Patti's stage ornaments) and
enamels and porcelain. Views and models of London
buildings through the ages, arid relics of criminals.
Something for all tastes surely!

I have a special weaknesss too, for the NATIONAL
PORTRAIT GALLERY. It is rather remarkable that such
a gallery should only exist in England, for what is
more natural and universal than the desire to see
what famous people looked like! It is not the quality
of the pictures (though there are quite a number of
good pictures there), but the people depicted which
makes this place so interesting. Blessed (for once) are
the harmless and simple-minded who care only for
what a picture represents! Have a look at Henry VIII's
wives, and see what you think of his taste. Decide
if Elizabeth could have been his daughter. Look at
the delicate and surprisingly "modern" face of "Bloody
Mary"; surely that woman was never deliberately
cruel; she simply had "nerves" and should have been
psycho-analysed. There are Elizabeth and Essex; there
are three Mary Stuarts, and very different she looks
in each picture; and there is a discovery to be made
here: Elizabeth was like Mary Stuart, thence their
hatred. There is the famous Shakespeare portrait, and
that of Bacon who "wrote him"; there are all the Stuarts,
who had charm, and there is Oliver Cromwell, who had
character; there are all the many lovely ladies Charles II
adored, painted by Lely, and among them Nell Gwynne,
ancestress of all the stars with "sex appeal." Meet—as
the films say—John Gay of the *Beggar's Opera*, all
the heavy Georges from Hanover, and Hogarth (self-
portrait) who caught the popular spirit of the times;
for if Gainsborough represents "Mayfair," Hogarth
represents the spirit of the Borough on Saturday night.
The later Royalty, alas! chose bad portraitists; they
found no Holbein or Vandyk. Take your choice between
Byron or Thackeray, Browning or Darwin, Disraeli or

Chamberlain, Aubrey Beardsley or Sir Henry Irving, busts or drawings. And when you are tired of the lot, you might amuse yourself by making out a list of contemporaries your children or grandchildren are likely to see here. . . .

DULWICH GALLERY is an unexpected result of the partition of Poland, for most of its pictures were collected by a dealer for Stanislas, who did not require them when he had to leave his kingdom; and it is very pleasantly situated in what is perhaps London's most charming suburb. There are some very good Dutch pictures there, including a famous Rembrandt; there are Watteaus, Murillos, Rubenses, and there is Reynolds' "Mrs. Siddons as the Tragic Muse," which will tell you more about the eighteenth-century notion of tragedy and of acting than you will ever learn from books. And while you are at Dulwich you might as well see the primitive or savage art treasures of the HORNIMAN MUSEUM, which London owes to tea—that is to say, to a tea merchant—while at the other end of London, beer— that is, Lord Iveagh—has presented her with KEN WOOD, the rooms of which are a delight, while the pictures are of varied merit.

Such, then, are London's museums; but what about London's living art, for a city may hold the most magnificent treasures and yet be quite dead as an art centre. Well, London is anything but dead, and it is a great art centre, though not in the sense that Paris is. To begin with, it is a most important picture market, and Europe's greatest picture dealers, such as Duveen or Colnaghi, live here. If very important collections come up for auction, the chances are that they will find their way to London and to Christie's, or to Sotheby's if they are books. The atmosphere of these London sale-rooms is remarkably different from Paris and Druot's. Druot's is a market, a huge, unaired place permanently overcrowded, where you may find anything from a torn old mattress to priceless treasures; Christie's is small, sombre, dignified and quiet, and you dare hardly enter it as an outsider. Art in England is to a far greater extent than in any other country an appanage of "Society,"; that is why sale-rooms, picture-dealers, antique shops have to be in London's most fashionable quarters. For many centuries England was exclusively a buyer of art; at present it is also a seller. New York buys art here, buys all the old English art it can get hold of. Until recently English art never got abroad—the works of Reynolds and Gainsborough and Raeburn remained here, and very often with the patrons whom these artists had worked for. Thence the enormous art-wealth of the country; but until recently the United States paid almost any price for English paintings, colour prints, furniture, of the eighteenth century in particular. The disdain of the art critics does not affect its high auction-room value, nor has the change of taste in architecture and interior decoration had much influence on it. The English themselves prefer their own art, their own furniture, to any other, and that is why the London art shops have a character of their own. If you except pictures, amongst which there will be many works of famous foreign painters, you will find little in them that is not English. You will see Chippendale chairs and Georgian silver and Stuart embroidery in shop after shop. Even in the smaller and less expensive shops, of which there are so many, all will be English; only where St. James's Street, King Street, Bond Street, or Wigmore Street will show works of the seventeenth and eighteenth centuries, Ebury Street, King's Road, etc., are full of cheaper Victorian stuff. Persian rugs and Chinese porcelain are among the very few "outsiders" definitely naturalised in England. You can find astounding things in London and an astounding variety of places where they are for sale—from the Caledonian Market, where it is not always advisable to inquire where the things come from, to shops so distinguished that you feel an address in Grosvenor Square and the possession of a Rolls-Royce are indispensable to anyone wishing to enter them.

That is London as an art market; but is London a centre of living, of modern art? Here, again, its position is peculiar. There have always been English artists, of course, since painting began (anew) in the eighteenth century, but nineteenth-century English painting has not interested other countries. There is the ROYAL ACADEMY, which goes on for ever, respected by the nation like the Church, the Law, or the Army, but laughed at in artistic circles. As its name implies, it is quite extraordinarily academic, a place where Sargent was considered a great revolutionary painter long after Cézanne's death. It is worth seeing, if only for the extraordinary old ladies to be found there; it has the most Victorian atmosphere in London. For some years now there have been most impressive exhibitions at the Academy, giving a survey of the art of one country after another. They are among the chief artistic events of the after-war period, for the most representative works of English and foreign public galleries and private collections were combined here; such were the shows of Dutch art, Flemish art, Italian art (particularly brilliant and successful), and Persian art, the latter really the first of its kind. But the Academy only lends its rooms to them. The NEW ENGLISH ART CLUB holds much the same position in London, and dates from about the same period as the *Société Nationale* in Paris or the *Sezession* in the German capitals; which means that it was new when the men over fifty were young revolutionaries, many of whom have now landed in the safe haven of the R.A.

There are many more recent groups, but none of them is representative of an entire generation or even of a definite movement. In London, as in other art centres, interest has shifted from the big shows to those arranged by picture-dealers, and the modern art movement must be studied in such galleries as the Lefèvre, Leicester, Tooth, and a few more. There are a good many interesting young English painters and sculptors: Duncan Grant, Matthew Smith, Dobson, and many others, but they are not yet known outside their own country. Paris is the centre of the great new art movement which is quite international in character, and it is in Paris that a young

Swede or Argentine, Spaniard or Japanese will become known to the world at large. But English painting continues to depend on the verdict of London, and to be bought by the English, who, on the other hand, show little interest in foreign art, except perhaps the French. So London as a centre of modern art is limited to the English; you will see work there which you can see nowhere else, and you will not find the work which you may safely look forward to seeing in any important gallery on the Continent or in New York. Modern art in London appeals to a small section only, but that section contains a sufficient number of patrons to keep art and artists alive. The masses still consider Epstein the very latest word in daring modernism, and whenever a new work of his is put up it provokes a "scandal"—whether it is his statuary on a Strand building, his "Rima," his work on the Underground Buildings, or his "Genesis." He is one of the most important of living sculptors, and would long have been considered a "Classic" abroad.

There is little general interest in "live"—that is, experimental—art in London, though one may sometimes come across it in unexpected places, such as the WHITE-CHAPEL ART GALLERY. But then "fine art" is of small importance to the masses in all countries nowadays. On the other hand, one should remember that this partitioning of fine and applied art is really a fatal nineteenth-century error; there is plenty of art (or artistic taste, if you prefer it) in the fabrics and furniture, china and cotton and woollen goods produced in England and shown in London shops. And London has one kind of artist quite peculiar to itself: the pavement artist, with his coloured chalks, who paints King George, battleships, landscapes, God knows what not, on the pavement, and always finds admirers or patrons willing to part with a copper. Some of these productions are quite extraordinary; they cannot be collected, but I would suggest a book of photographic reproductions to some enterprising publisher.

85   PAVEMENT ARTIST, HYDE PARK CORNER

86   CHRISTMAS TOYS IN HOLBORN

87   MUSIC HALL: Gracie Fields

CHAPTER VI

LONDON AMUSEMENTS AND NIGHT LIFE

LONDON has many theatres, but I cannot say how many, nor does the number mean very much. The West End has about forty theatres which produce plays, but quite a number of others which may show plays to-day and films or revues or variety to-morrow, and all the new houses are built to suit either plays or films. The number of suburban theatres is also very great, and they do not as a rule advertise in the papers. Whittaker puts the total number (excluding cinemas) at about a hundred, but then again, while some suburban theatres have a character of their own, others are really "provincial" and toured by companies from "London" —that is, the West End. London is quite different from Paris, Berlin, or Vienna, where most theatres have a definite character of their own. There a theatre may belong to, let us say, Max Reinhardt, or at least he may have a lease of many years, but in London most theatres belong to business men who let them to producers for a season or for the run of a play; so that you may see a musical comedy to-day on the stage where you saw Shakespeare last week. In pre-war days the actor-manager was a feature: Irving, Tree, George Alexander, all had their theatres and their permanent companies, but at present actors are generally engaged for the run of one play only, which may be produced in whatever theatre happens to be available, though there are just a few "stars" more definitely associated with one particular house.

The old houses have retained a certain amount of tradition. COVENT GARDEN is associated with opera, and it is indeed the typical opera-house of the time of Italian opera, with its many tiers of closed-in boxes. It is Italian also in that it is only open for a *stagione*, a summer season of three months, and possibly an autumn season. Opera has a strange fate in London. Covent Garden is as old-

O

fashioned as it is charming; it continues to attract great singers (in German, Italian, French, or even English) and conductors, but its staging is incurably 1880. Before the war a splendid and very up-to-date opera-house was built in Kingsway, but it did not pay and is now a cinema. Opera has never become democratised in England, but that is not because the public is "un-musical" (there could not be the very many excellent concerts if that were the case), but because it is very conservative, and because opera is aristocratic and a Court show in its origin. Everywhere opera was origin-ally subsidised by the Court and patronised by Court society; it was part of that social life. But on the Con-tinent, particularly in Germany, the bourgeoisie followed suit, and opera there is run by the State or the muni-cipality and subsidised by the taxpayers, so that they naturally regard it as their own. In England, however, though Covent Garden is not subsidised by the Crown, it is not subsidised by State or County Council either, but a season is a private enterprise, the costs for which (for opera has a deficit all over the world) are born by members of Society. In 1931 for the first time the Government granted a small subsidy to Covent Garden, a decision much criticised, and not surprisingly so when you remember that even most hospitals depend on "voluntary contributions" in England. So Covent Garden has remained associated with the Season and with Society, with dress and jewellery and the *grand monde*—an eighteenth-century conception.

That the masses are fond of opera is shown by the success of the OLD VIC, now run partly as a People's Opera, where the charges are very moderate. Its per-formances are excellent—considering. There are some touring opera companies, provincial in character, and there is always a movement on foot for a "National Opera," but I doubt whether it will ever lead to much.

Quite near Covent Garden stands the THEATRE ROYAL, DRURY LANE (to give it its full title), for this is the old theatrical centre of London, following the Shakespearean which was on the Surrey side, outside

88   GALLERY QUEUE

89   FIRST NIGHT AUDIENCE

the City boundaries. It is a huge building in the classical style of 1812, but its interior has recently been modernised out of all recognition, and is now comfortable and of no character. It is the fourth building on this same site. Here the great tragedians of the eighteenth century acted Shakespeare: Garrick, Mrs. Siddons, etc.; there is a statue of Shakespeare inside the theatre still, but that is all its connection with him now. If Drury Lane still has a tradition, it dates from Victorian times, and is one of spectacular melodrama. It provides a "great show" and the traditional Christmas "pantomime," and it holds 2,600 spectators. The LYCEUM close by, the third of the three historic houses, is even larger, for it holds 3,000. This was Shakespeare's temple in Irving's time, but now it mostly shows melodrama, and is as much as its neighbour a theatre for the masses. There are a few more theatres in this district, but of no particular character, though, of course, any one of them may at any time become of interest.

In Victorian times the Strand and Aldwych were London's theatre and amusement centre, but of late times this has shifted westward. Quite lately, however, the Strand theatres have been rejuvenating themselves, and two of them, the ADELPHI and the SAVOY, are now amongst the most modern in decoration, while the WHILTEHALL Theatre is one of the last to be opened. The GAIETY, ALDWYCH, and STRAND Theatres also are by no means antiquated, but the Gaiety is no longer what it was in pre-war times when it occupied a position similar to that of the VARIÉTÉS in Paris, and its chorus-girls became peeresses. The smart world that used to crowd it has gone over to Cochran's shows, his revues at the LONDON PAVILION and other ventures, while Charlot's revues or plays come a good second. The huge new DOMINION THEATRE, built to house 2,900 at low prices, was intended for musical comedy shows, but became a cinema after a very few months. The centre of stage-land at present lies west of Trafalgar Square. St. Martin's Lane has two theatres beside the huge COLISEUM, the Charing Cross Road four or five, another

five are in Shaftesbury Avenue, two lie in Soho, and
half a dozen in and around St. James's, while the cinemas
are almost numberless. Only a very few of these theatres
have any tradition. There is HIS MAJESTY'S, with
memories of Tree and Shakespeare, and the distinguished Georgian HAYMARKET THEATRE opposite, and
the ST. JAMES'S THEATRE where productions are always
up to a certain standard, and perhaps the PLAYHOUSE,
when Gladys Cooper is there with one of the light and
clever Society comedies London specialises in. At all
the others anything may be produced, and the Londoner
does not yet attach himself to any particular theatre,
but goes to see certain actors, certain producers' efforts,
and sometimes even a certain play—no matter where he
finds them.

I think that the level of acting has never been as high
in London as it is at present. Like everywhere else there
are no real "stars," though quite a number of actors or
actresses go by that name; there are no Irvings, Bern-
hardts, Duses on the post-war stage, but on the other
hand the general level is higher. London has quite a
number of remarkable dramatic actors, such as Mrs.
Patrick Campbell, Sybil Thorndike, Henry Ainley,
Gielgud, or Charles Laughton, and an extraordinary
number of comediennes (there is no English term),
like Marie Tempest, Yvonne Arnaud, Edith Evans, Gwen
ffrangcon-Davies, Gladys Cooper, Tallulah Bankhead,
Isabel Jeans, Gertrude Lawrence. It is richest of all, however, in actors of musical comedy or farce, such as Jack
Buchanan, Jack Hulbert, Leslie Henson, Evelyn Laye,
Cicely Courtneidge, Gracie Fields, Ivy St. Helier, or music-
hall comedians like George Robey and Ernie Lotinga—
a most incomplete list of truly remarkable artists.
Nowhere are farce or light comedy better acted, but here,
again, you may find a perfect ensemble and discreet and
subtle acting in one theatre, and find that next door
a company holds the stage which might consist of
amateurs of the year 1880. Still more a matter of chance
is the quality of the plays to be seen at any particular
moment; you may find four theatres producing *Hamlet*

(which happened in 1930) and two more acting Shakespeare, or there may be no Shakespeare anywhere. There may be excellent plays by Shaw, Maugham, Lonsdale, Coward, all on at the same time, or there may be nothing but "thrillers" and idiotic musical comedy shows. A play like *Journey's End* may become a huge success, and the next success will be the worst play in the world, with some actor or actress who happens to be the rage. Such is the theatre life of the West End, which is supposed to stand for all London.

But London's theatre life is not so simple a matter, and, just as some of its architectural treasures lie hidden in odd corners, while the great thoroughfares may have little to boast of, so there are many stage surprises in unexpected places. Amongst these pride of place belongs to the OLD VIC, with which is now associated SADLER'S WELLS. The "Old Vic," where they mostly do Shakespeare and opera, is situated in a very poor quarter, the Borough, where once Shakespeare acted, while Sadler's Wells is in a rather similar district of northern London —Islington. They will come as a great surprise to those who are accustomed to judge the English stage by the West End only. Drama had never gone out of favour with that public which frequents the theatres and halls of the Borough and similar London districts, only it had sunk to the level of crudest melodrama. But when some people were bold enough to give that public Shakespeare instead, the response was instantaneous, nor has it ever wavered since. So here you have Shakespeare acted before a public very similar to that for which he wrote his plays, though it is partly a "cultured" audience as well, that is to say, in the dearer seats. The repertoire of the "Old Vic" and of Sadler's Wells includes other classics and opera, modern plays too occasionally; and they are real "people's theatres," though no political party or society bent on improving the mind of the masses stand behind them.

Another outstanding success was the *Beggar's Opera*. Here, again, it has been proved that the public responds to good plays well acted in any part of London, for the *Beggar's Opera*, staged at Hammersmith, broke all London records. There are several other suburban theatres whose standard is high. As their rents are probably low, they can afford to experiment with modern plays which the West End fears as too intellectual. Of such are the EMBASSY Theatre at Swiss Cottage and the WESTMINSTER Theatre by Victoria Station. The East End has its Yiddish PAVILION Theatre, where the acting is often superb. And finally one must not overlook the STAGE SOCIETIES. They are private, and thus not subject to censorship, so they can and do produce a very great number of plays which would never see the footlights without them. They have been very instrumental in raising the standard of taste, and many of the plays tried out here have been taken on by West End theatres later. Sometimes they have their own stages, such as the Arts Theatre, Gate Theatre, etc. Their productions are almost invariably interesting, and as membership is neither costly nor difficult, people interested in serious drama have good opportunities for seeing it in London. Nor should one forget the very many amateur dramatic societies, for though their shows are not public, they also prove how very great is the interest in the drama in London and in all England. The English stage is very alive, in spite of all pessimistic accounts, only one must take the trouble to discover that life for oneself.

The London Music-halls are unique. Many have disappeared, but those left are better than anything similar elsewhere. The COLISEUM has given up variety, it seems, while the ALHAMBRA has reverted to it, and there is still the huge PALLADIUM where you may see or hear Gracie Fields or Sophie Tucker, Jack Hylton's Band or Russian Ballet, with the best of acrobats, jugglers and comedians. But it is the smaller and more local houses which are most typically English, like the HOLBORN EMPIRE or the halls of Edgware Road or Chelsea, and a number of suburban ones. Here the English comedian still rules supreme; you may see the great George Robey or Ernie Lotinga, and these "clowns" represent perhaps the most traditionally and

91   THEATRE TURNED CINEMA, LEICESTER SQUARE

92   EYES LEFT! A Football Audience at Highbury

93   EYES RIGHT! A Cabaret Audience in the West End

characteristically English type on the stage. Charlie Chaplin has transferred it to the screen, and his films belong to all the world. London has innumerable cinemas, and they are no different to those of other towns all the world over. Most are very luxurious, in the American taste or tastelessness, some like the NEW VICTORIA, SHEPHERD'S BUSH, and other suburban houses are architecturally remarkable, but the most amusing ones are the cheap little old-fashioned ones (in Tottenham Court Road, for instance), now often converted into "News Reels." Theatres, music-halls, and cinemas are all extremely comfortable compared to the continental average, and there is a pleasant absence of fuss or dishonest speculation about the whole business of going to the play. There are heaps of offices all over London where you can get the best seats obtainable, and these will not be snapped up by speculators if a play is a success, as in Paris. There are no fussy *ouvreuses* demanding tips, and the County Council sees to it that there are plenty of exits. The cloakrooms, on the other hand, are very poor, and most people prefer to avoid the frightful delay they entail. Quite apart from the play, an evening spent in a London theatre is pleasant on account of the people who take the trouble to dress, the comfortable seats and the well-mannered attendants.

The cabaret has taken on a peculiar form in London. It does not exist as an independent entertainment, but only in conjunction with supper and dancing at many of the big hotels or expensive supper places. The Café de Paris, Café Anglais, Piccadilly, Trocadero, and a number of others provide a cabaret show. Generally there are only a small number of entertainers, but these are of the very first rank, like Douglas Byng, Hutch, Sophie Tucker, and some of the exhibition dancers. The cabaret is, in fact, the connecting link between "the stage" and "night life." It is well known that London has extraordinarily little night life compared with any other (non-English) capital. There are many reasons for this, the chief, of course, being the licensing laws, which will not allow drink after 11 or 12 p.m. This would be a drawback anywhere, but it is more so in England than it would be abroad, where people care less for drink. Next there are the enormous distances to be considered, which prevent the vast majority, who have come home late and tired from their work, from venturing out on more long journeys. This rules out the greater part of the middle-class population. London's night life is limited to very small sections of its huge population: the so-called Society people (or rather a part of that self-termed class), Bohemians, foreign visitors, and the shady elements. All these are provided for.

The smart people go up and sup at the Berkeley or Claridge's or the Savoy, the Café Anglais or Café de Paris, dance a little and see a few star turns, unless they prefer the more exclusive supper-clubs like the Embassy or Ciro's. There you will see many well-known people, many smart dresses and good-looking women, but their very exclusiveness makes them more like private entertainments than anything else. There is no mixture of classes, no element of surprise, no cosmopolitan atmosphere. Bohemia and the smart people (both sets overlap), many actors or artists and writers may be found at the Savoy Grill or smaller restaurants and night clubs round Soho, but their chief diversion is the giving and visiting of private parties, of which there is no end, from the simplest to the very elaborate. For such is London life: nearly everything worth while is a private concern, is exclusive in some way: clubs or night clubs, parties, Royal or other enclosures at the races, Ranelagh or' Hurlingham for sports; and while this system has many advantages for the included, the excluded cannot be expected to enjoy it, and to the excluded naturally belong all foreign tourists, who are therefore inclined to pronounce London at night an extremely dull place.

The shady elements of central London, of Soho, Seven Dials, Tottenham Court Road, lead a life of insecure gaiety at night-clubs continually raided by the police, closed down, and reopened a few doors farther on. It is a shifting and shifty sort of a game.

All that side of London life seems to me purely de-

94   BOXING AT THE WHITE CITY

95   PARIS IN REGENT STREET

pressing and sordid. Such people must and do exist in every great capital; they are, whether you like it or not, part of white civilisation, but public opinion refuses to recognise and face this fact, and all sorts of expedients are resorted to instead. On the whole I should say that there is less of this in London than in former times, and I should say the same about Paris—a fact I do not attribute to any increase in virtue, but rather to a stricter police supervision, and also in part to the changed moral code of the women of the bourgeois class. But no matter how that may be, one thing is certain, and that is that the London "haunts of vice" have little of the attractiveness of similar places abroad. Foreign visitors find little to amuse them in London once the theatres are closed; there are no cafés (strange to think that the coffee-houses flourished in London at one time), they cannot get into a club, the supper places open to them close early, and so they go home and report that London is hopelessly boring, which is one reason why London attracts so very few continental visitors. It has a vast number of visitors from the provinces, the Dominions, and colonies, and from the United States (though in-finitely more Americans go to Paris), but visitors from the Continent come to London mainly for business, possibly once in their life for sight-seeing—but not for pleasure. There is no denying the truth that the night entertainments of London which are public cannot compete with those of continental capitals. There are dancing and supper places, but only the lesser fry frequent them, and they are not very impressive; there are skating-rinks, but here, again, the best are clubs. There are Lyons' Corner Houses, very admirable in their way, but not built for the pleasure-seeking tourist. Then, worst of all, there are no open-air entertainments in summer. London has lost Earl's Court, the White City, Wembley; at the same time there is hardly a trace of a café where one can sit out at night, and the parks are closed early. There is nowhere for the people to go except to the cinemas. If London or England wished to be a strictly puritan country this would be logical, but

P

as they now spend a good deal of money on advertising to attract tourist traffic it is anything but logical.

London is now very well off for music. It has excellent orchestral concerts under all great foreign or English conductors, and all the famous *virtuosi* can be heard. It has choral festivals, and some of the English choirs are world-famous; it has also excellent lighter music and dance-bands, while its musical comedy productions are most efficient. But much the same might be said of any great city nowadays, for musicians are travelling folk.

CHAPTER VII
LONDON HOTELS AND RESTAURANTS

Every guide-book contains a more or less complete list of the hotels and restaurants of the city, described, but if it distinguishes some by a star, or even more, it says little about their character and atmosphere. It is true that hotels of any particular character are getting very scarce since they are rapidly becoming exactly alike all the world over. This has become very noticeable since the war, though it had begun to be true long before it, and nowadays all the earth is covered with "Palaces" exactly alike and often belonging to some international company. They may be very perfect, but it is certain that a person conducted to one of them blindfolded after having been dropped from an aeroplane could not tell whether he was in the lounge, bar, or dining-room of a "Palace" of London, Paris, Madrid, or Rome. I think the modern hotel was originally an English invention, for the very idea of specialised rooms for different purposes came to the Continent from England. Versailles only knew *salons*, in some of which it served meals and in some of which it put state beds, but the bedroom furnished as such, the dining-room, later the smoking-room, bathroom, billiard-room, nursery, etc., are English inventions. In the same way, the demands of English travellers transformed continental hotels, which had formerly hardly known public rooms. In the nineteenth century England's hotels were "modern" when others were old-fashioned, and for that same reason they are now largely old-fashioned compared with those of continental cities, where modernism arrived later. In the last few years a considerable number of new hotels has sprung up in London, but the average London hotel is old-fashioned compared with those of the Continent, and still more, of course, with those of America. Any small Paris hotel has hot and cold running water, central heating, lifts, and a number of rooms with bathrooms attached, while the small London hotel has remained unchanged for the last twenty-five years.

There are a number of categories of hotels in London, beginning with the *de luxe* hotel (quite a horrible designation, by the way), which is a cosmopolitan palace of no great individuality. But there are slight differences even here. The SAVOY has an atmosphere of its own, a slight air of expensive bohemianism. Its grill-room is so placed that you actually see the people sitting in it from outside, and that is almost unique in London, where people in restaurants are concealed from the gaze of the profane as if they were at divine service. The Savoy manages to hide the fact that it is huge, and to appear cosy; it has a fine view over the river from its dining-room, and an odd metallic courtyard facing the Strand. People go there to amuse themselves, and the Savoy manages to mix different classes of people, which is seldom achieved (or perhaps seldom aimed at) in London. The BERKELEY has an air of smartness with a faint eighteenth-century touch about it (though it is quite modern), which is very Mayfairish. London has very few *de luxe* hotels compared with Paris, but it has placed them in enviable situations, for if you wish to overlook wide stretches of park you have the Ritz, the Hyde Park, the Splendide, Grosvenor House, the Dorchester, and the Kensington Palace Hotel (with the widest view of all) to choose from, while the Savoy has its river.

Most of these are modern buildings, but the typical Victorian hotel is not of that sort. The majority of the large London hotels were built in late Victorian times, and they are not "modern" any longer, but pleasant enough in their way, and certainly more characteristically English than their successors. Those were "spacious times," which means that the commercial value of space was disregarded, and so you find huge high bedrooms and colossal public rooms with monumental furniture in these places. They all seem modelled on Renascence palaces, just like the clubs or banks of that period.

They offer solid comfort, look heavy and even gloomy, have an air of eminent respectability but also a kind of dignity which newer places lack. They are, in fact, English, while the new hotels all the world over were built after American taste had begun to rule. Possibly they may have succumbed to jazz and cocktails, but one certainly does not associate these with the ponderous and blackened massiveness of hotels like the GROSVENOR, VICTORIA, METRO POLE, LANGHAM, or the big station hotels. They stand for tea and crumpets and huge breakfasts and massive silver dishes. Their heyday is, alas! over. The CHARING CROSS HOTEL used to be a sombre home of romance when trains left there for "Europe," and eloping couples and cashiers and would-be suicides favoured it; while now people stay there who like to be quiet. There are a few hotels of the same period in Mayfair, of a character adapted to that neigh-bourhood as it was then, like BROWN'S or BATT'S, strongholds of the "landed gentry" which came up for the Season, and which greeted "outsiders" with raised eyebrows. But if there are thus many "period" hotels in London, there are hardly any "historic" ones, for it takes a century to transform the former into the latter. I can only think of WILLIAMSON'S HOTEL in Bow Lane, and of the ADELPHI.

At a slightly later period than the last described, Bloomsbury blossomed forth as a hotel district, and Norfolk Street, Strand and the adjoining streets, with their comfortable pseudo-Tudor, must date from much the same time. Bloomsbury offers every variety of habita-tion for strangers known to London, and London knows more varieties than any other city, and a bewildering nomenclature. There is the "bed-and-breakfast house," there are "apartments," there are "chambers," there are "service flats," etc. But chief of all there is the "board-ing-house," sometimes called "private hotel" (quite senselessly, I think), a very British institution indeed. Bloomsbury is by no means its only home, for it clusters thickly north of Hyde Park, and at Ladbroke Grove farther west, but I think Bloomsbury must have the largest selection. The English boarding-house is an essentially middle-class institution; that is why everyone there is intensely class-conscious. They have an atmosphere of decayed gentility, which includes the owner, and the types to be met there never seem to vary, for you will find them in Thackeray's very amusing *Book of Snobs* as in the not less amusing twentieth-century comedy *At Mrs. Beam's*, by Hector Munro. To the purely British types Bloomsbury adds American tourists, cultured and sight-seeing, and foreign city clerks learning English. Each house has a formidable old lady monopolising the fire, who is related to somebody or other, a crusty old bachelor rumoured to be a wealthy miser, and every variety of elderly spinster. They are a rather absurd and also a very pathetic lot, because they are nearly all people who fear living alone or who cannot afford a home. That is why the *milieu* always appeals to satirists, and also to more tender souls, like the author of *The Third Floor Back*.

Bloomsbury is also the home of the "Temperance Hotel," but I think they are mostly not so puritan and high-principled as a continental visitor might fear or hope, but simply cannot obtain a licence. Then there are the huge modern hotels which are extraordinarily cheap and completely standardised, like the elderly American lady tourists or younger commercial travellers who frequent them. The most splendid specimens of these hotels have been provided by Lyons (not in Bloomsbury though), and his "Palaces" are as fantastic creations as his "Corner Houses." Here is "luxury for the masses" indeed at cheap and uniform prices; there are no tips, and everything is strictly standardised. You get all a *de luxe* offers, and more; palatial surroundings with any amount of marble and gilt and light, and sometimes the decorative scheme is very good too; there are reading-rooms and writing-rooms, rooms for billiards and for smoking; there is a grill and a restaurant and a barber's shop and a post-office and chemists' stalls and newspaper and cigarette-stalls, and there is a gargantuan entrance-hall. It is always crammed with people, with neat and bustling waitresses, page-boys yelling numbers, bands playing brassy Wagner or Puccini. The crowd is as remarkable in its way as the Royal Academy crowd in another, for it seems to be composed of people you see nowhere else in London: massive provincials, the oddest old ladies, lusty youths in plus fours, Hindus, Jews, people of all colours and races, of all continents and even from the European Continent, all seemingly enjoying themselves hugely twenty-four hours of the day. One of London's great sights in fact.

Thus London's extraordinary variety shows itself in its hotels as in everything else. You may find them small, none too modern, but very expensive around Bond Street, or huge and modern and twice as comfortable at half the price—but there you are; they cater for different classes. You will find absolutely banal and cosmopolitan hotels, and others where you will be suspect if you do not have bacon and eggs for breakfast; you will find solid comfort and high-class respectability, reminiscent of broughams and well-fed horses, in one place, and rattling windows and a broken water-jug on a rickety stand in another; you will find (again a speciality of London) hotels which have been beautiful country houses with large parks and golf courses, and others in some dingy side-street of dismal appearance. And it is most remarkable perhaps that in most districts you will not find any hotels at all.

Much of what has been said about hotels applies to restaurants equally. There is a greater variety of restaurants in London than in any other European capital except Paris, and they can be divided into much the same categories. All the *de luxe* hotels are at the same time restaurants, and they are exactly like the same type all over the world. The Savoy Grill is amusing for supper, the Berkeley for lunch, but these things are liable to change, and fashion may just as well have adopted other places of the kind by the time these lines appear in print. The last years have seen the rise of a number of small and invariably foreign restaurants, or in some cases clubs, highly in favour at present. A few years ago they all bore French names like BOULESTIN'S; now they are all Italian. Probably you cannot find better food or more eccentric dishes anywhere in the world at present than at places like SOVRANI'S or QUAGLINO'S, unless it is at the EMBASSY CLUB or at CIRO'S. They are distinguished from similar restaurants in Paris not by their food but by their public, for here it is essentially English, while there it is mainly "foreign" (not French). There is also the fact that while in Paris the small restaurant with famous food is an ancient institution, it is a new one to London.

As there are Victorian hotels, so there are restaurants with the same atmosphere. Late Victorian times saw the rise of the enormous eating-houses around Piccadilly Circus of a type peculiar to London like the CRITERION, the TROCADERO, MONICO, CAFÉ ROYAL. Each of these heavy stone mansions really contains a number of restaurants, grills, bars, cafés, etc. The rooms or halls are huge and high, in every way different from the small intimate modern places. They are the paradises of provincials, foreigners, and the solid bourgeoisie. The food is good, if on the solid side, though the Café Royal was long famous for its cuisine and cellar, and also contains about the only restaurant in London corresponding to a continental café. It has been a famous artists' gathering-place, but when it was rebuilt and its gilt and mirrors and plush disappeared, much of its character vanished with them. There are some similar food mansions farther east: the HOLBORN and FRASCATI'S, and ROMANO'S in the Strand, the last of which attracts many stage people.

Though English cooking has a bad reputation, this is really unfounded, but the trouble is that you get it at comparatively few places only. There are a few well-known and typically English restaurants: SIMPSON'S, with its pageant of beef, SCOTT'S with its lobsters of monumental size, PIM'S in the City; and there is RULE'S in Maiden Lane, with its wonderful Victorian alabaster

96   SALOON BAR

97   EUSTON ROAD SNACK COUNTER

98   YE OLDE LUNCHE IN FLEET STREET

groups against a plush background, and its colour-prints—a most delightful place. There is the famous CHESHIRE CHEESE, unfortunately overrun by sightseers; there are BIRCH'S, and SIMPSON'S in Bird-in-Hand Court, with its "fish-ordinary" and ancient custom of "guessing the weight of the cheese." But apart from these famous places, you can get very excellent English food at nearly all the big public-houses like the HORSE SHOE in Tottenham Court Road, the GARRICK in Leicester Square, DE HEMS off Shaftesbury Avenue, etc., all of which are comfortable, very good in their way, and very typical of London. Altogether I think that the London "pubs" are far too little visited by foreigners; indeed, they are largely left to the lower classes by the English themselves, but they are much more interesting and curious than other and smarter drinking-places. The American bars of the Carlton, Mayfair, etc., are in no way different from similar bars in Paris, Berlin, or Rome, but the mahogany and shining brass and advertisement mirrors of the "pubs" are to be found nowhere else. Nowhere else do you see thirsty queues lined up waiting for the opening hour, and children playing in the street while the parents refresh themselves; nowhere else do they divide a bar into a number of partitions (thus creating the class distinctions the British love), and nowhere else do you find a similar atmosphere of good-humoured fellowship. I find the ones I know very cheerful places, but it would need a lifetime to know all and a volume to describe them. At the FITZROY TAVERN (adopted by the artists of the neighbourhood), the PLOUGH near the British Museum, the HORSE SHOE in Tottenham Court Road, the DUNCANNON at Charing Cross, and many others the names of which I have forgotten, I have always found cheerful people, and not very many drunk, and if they should be I am inclined to agree with Byron: "Man, being reasonable, must get drunk"—occasionally at least. All the same, I admit that I deplore the absence of cafés of the continental type in London, for they are places to dwell in, where "pubs" are only pleasant for a short time. I would put cafés into all the

Q

squares, and along the Embankment, and wherever else there is room for them; and I am sure this would be most beneficial both to sobriety and to English literature. But it seems ordained that you can have either cafés or clubs, but that both do not flourish under the same sky.

If, however, the continental visitor misses cafés, he need not miss his native cuisine, no matter which it may be, for the foreign restaurants of London are innumerable, and almost every nation is represented, and well represented. Soho is a sort of permanent exhibition of foreign cooking. The French would really need no restaurants of their own, for every first-class restaurant in London (as everywhere else) has a French cuisine, but there are small French restaurants all the same, like JULES' in Jermyn Street, or L'ESCARGOT in Soho. The Italians have PAGANI'S (with its Caruso souvenirs) and the ISOLA BELLA and the TAVERNA MEDICEA, so true to its name that they give you three-pronged forks; of the Spanish the most famous is MARTINEZ in Swallow Street, while South America has descended upon Greek Street. Germans and Austrians can go to ODDENINO'S or APPENRODT'S or SCHMIDT'S, Hungarians to the HUNGARIA, Russians to the KASBEK, and lots of others. The Chinese have MAXIM'S where yellow and white dance together, the Indians VEERASAWMY'S, with its white-clad silent waiters and its highly curried dishes, and these are but a few names amongst many. There is a little street I know near Soho where Americans, Greeks and Negroes all have their resorts adjoining each other.

Those who are frightened of foreign food and wish to eat cheaply have big and rather nondescript places at their disposal, like SLATER'S or FLEMING'S, and the restaurants of the big stores, and of course there is the providential LYONS'. Lyons' always makes me feel cynical; he (or it) is a Napoleon of catering. Lyons' owns huge hotels, equally huge places devoted entirely to food, others which do not bear his name, and as to his "cafés," there seems to be one in every other house of the big thoroughfares, so that other organisations, like the "A.B.C." or EXPRESS DAIRIES, appear almost insignificant by comparison. A Lyons' cafe is a thing by itself, neither a café in the continental sense nor a British teashop nor a restaurant nor a confectioner's, but a little of each. It is very cheap, clean, efficient, and it has neat and mostly smiling waitresses. But it also gives you a numbing feeling of being no more than a number; a million waitresses serve a million similar pots of tea and pieces of cake to a million customers who ought to be as alike as the pots. But Lyons' great marvel (apart from his hotels) are his CORNER HOUSES. The best known is that in Coventry Street, with its six floors (or are there more?) of buffets and restaurants, of marble and mirrors, barber's shop and telephone cells; with its ground-floor shops which sell flowers and chocolates and God knows what, its orchestras around every corner, and its never-ceasing torrent of customers. England is the contrary to a socialist country, but it seems to me that the Corner House might well be a socialist State institution. The most awe-inspiring is the one in the Tottenham Court Road, really lovely in lighting and partly in decoration, a dazzling medley of glass, nickel, and marble. I remember it advertising its opening "for ever," for a Corner House stays open all night. If it were situated in Moscow one would read glowing accounts of what had been done for "the masses," for here there is more splendour than in real palaces, there are orgies of light and marble and music—and all for people who consume a 4d. cup of coffee. Thus between a "pub," a Ritz, and a Corner House you can find all imaginable types of restaurant in London, and I do not know where else you would find them together.

Curiously enough, though tea is the national beverage, London never had many smart *thés* like Paris. There are well-known confectioners' shops, like RUMPEL-MAYER'S, FULLER'S, STEWART'S, GUNTER'S, for tea and luncheon as well, which are quite feminine, but neither smart nor particularly amusing. Much more fun are the sandwich and snack bars now springing up everywhere.

This new development began with SANDY'S in Oxendon Street, which advertises one hundred and twenty varieties of sandwich. I feel it would be a noble task to try them all amid the pretty minor stage stars of both sexes who forgather there. All the neighbourhood of Leicester Square and Piccadilly Circus is now full of similar places under varying designations, and there is a particularly pleasant one in Denman Street. The sandwich is to me one of Britain's glories, and its inventor, the Earl of that name, one of the great benefactors of mankind, for anywhere they provide a quick and agreeable meal, in "pubs" or teashops or at *Delikatessen* stores; nor do I think the bad reputation of the railway sandwich at all merited.

One might spend an unlimited and not unentertaining time sampling all the different food London offers, and the different places it offers it in; from Scott's to an East End fried fish shop, from a cocktail at Claridge's to a half-pint in a "pub" of the Commercial Road, from lunch at Quaglino's to a "joint and two veg." at a shilling in a small chop-house, from supper at the Savoy to a cup of coffee and cake at one of the coffee-stalls which appear at night at the traffic centres, which have their habitués quite as much as the Embassy, and are at least as entertaining to the student of human nature.

99   MAYFAIR BUTCHER'S SHOP

100   WORKMEN'S DINING-ROOMS

101　2 A.M. AT HYDE PARK CORNER

102　LONDON'S NIGHTLY WASH: A Scene at the Law Courts

103   LITTLE ITALY IN CLERKENWELL

104   THE EARLY HOURS AT COVENT GARDEN

105   THE CHURCH AND THE LAW

CHAPTER VIII

TRADITIONAL LONDON

ONE cannot hope to understand London without considering its clubs, for they play an important part in the life of men, and women too. The Club is an essentially English institution, and it does not really flourish anywhere outside England. The chief prop of the club idea is the English class system. It is not true that the Englishman dislikes life in public and prefers to spend his leisure hours in his own home, but it is true that he dislikes promiscuity—at least in his own country. All English society is based on distinction of class. A French or a German boy will go to a *Lycée* if he belongs to the upper classes, where tuition is as good as free, and where he will meet boys of all other classes except those of the working class, where parents cannot afford to leave them at school after their fourteenth year. But he will be together with the butcher's son and the hairdresser's, the doctor's and the lawyer's and the small tradesman's, as well as with boys of his own class, and he will get used to spending his time in the society of people of all classes, just as he will continue to do during his service in the Army. The English boy of the upper classes goes to a Public School, which, if only on account of the expense entailed, is open only to the sons of well-to-do people, and so he grows used to a one-class society, and feels comfortable in no other. English society tends to strict class division, as does German to division by professions. The second prop of the club idea is, then, the public school system. Boys leave home at an early age to live at school, and there they get used to the idea of an all-masculine society. This is indeed a characteristic of all Germanic races as opposed to Latins, and the German *Stammtisch* or *Studentenverbindung* are as characteristic in that way as the English clubs. The result of being trained to the society of the same class and the same sex only is quite naturally that the boy continues to prefer it in later life, or at any rate does not wish to do without it. He does not want to spend all his time with men of his own class, but a good deal of it, and while this does not apply to all Englishmen, it does to the majority of the upper classes. Hence the Club.

The first social clubs grew out of the coffee-houses, for the eighteenth-century coffee-houses were primarily men's meeting-grounds. There are any amount of such purely social clubs, as BOODLE'S, WHITE'S, BROOKS'S, the COCOA TREE, the BACHELORS', the SAVILE, etc., all subtly distinguished in character if not in social status. Others go by profession as well as class, as the UNITED SERVICE, the ARMY AND NAVY, the GUARDS', and other Service clubs, the ATHENAEUM for men of learning, divines, eminent public men (obviously a very exclusive place), the ST. JAMES'S and the ORLEANS for diplomats, and the GREEN ROOM and the GARRICK for actors—or at least originally so. Then there are the famous clubs connected with sport: the BADMINTON for coaching and horses, RANELAGH and HURLINGHAM for polo, ROE-HAMPTON for golf, the LEANDER for rowing, the NATIONAL SPORTING CLUB for boxing, the PORTLAND for card games, and the huge ROYAL AUTOMOBILE CLUB. There are the very important political clubs: the CARLTON and JUNIOR CARLTON for the Conservatives, the NATIONAL LIBERAL and REFORM for the progressives; the clubs like the TRAVELLERS', the SAVAGE, the ECCEN-TRIC, which to some extent indicate their character by their names, though that must not be taken too literally. To this very incomplete list must be added all the ladies' clubs, but it does not, of course, include any of the purely sporting clubs which have their parallel abroad.

The clubs alluded to here are all social clubs, in spite of their distinctions, and nearly all have their houses, which might be called palaces without any exaggeration. At the very least they have a restaurant, mostly excellent, and thus a very large section of the upper classes habitu-ally take their meals in clubs. This is especially true of luncheon; while the City lunches largely at restaurants (though here also, there are clubs, including a City Carlton), the West End lunches chiefly in clubs—and this applies to both sexes. The clubs and their hospitality therefore play a great part in social life. To a great many men their club means home, for a great many are partly residential, and bachelors or men from the colonies or up from the provinces prefer to live there rather than in hotels or flats. Needless to say the club serves many other purposes: reading, correspondence, cards, and most of all keeping in touch with a number of people on half-neutral ground.

For an outsider or a tourist the existence of the clubs is regrettable, because they inevitably distract from the brilliance of restaurants, hotels, public life in general. But that is the character of London and of England all over: whatever is best is hidden and made difficult of access—which is, I think, the chief reason why most foreigners who know the country superficially do not like it, while nearly all who have lived there for some time do not want to leave it. But whatever the club may mean to the foreigner, to the Londoner it is of the greatest advantage, and really a club is a much pleasanter place than a café or a restaurant, and will continue to be so the noisier and more hectic life becomes.

Yet it is a pity that the clubs are so very private. All clubmen will probably be horror-stricken at so impertinent a suggestion, but I wish the clubs could be obliged to open their doors to the public on certain days, for there are so very many interesting things to be seen there. Some of the oldest members (and still more surely some of the grand servants) might die of shame, but it would incidentally improve the clubs' finances. A great part of London's treasures of art and of books are hidden in clubs, far less accessible than most private collections. Of course nearly all admit visitors if invited by a member, though here, again, the rules vary, some admitting only men, others women as well, some allowing them the entry to certain rooms only, while the Carlton has a special annex for visitors, and rigorously excludes them from its main building. Generally speaking, however, the public never enters any of them, and most of their interiors are not even known by photographs!

Most Londoners know the beautiful or imposing façades, the most charming of which I think that of BOODLE'S, though BROOKS'S might be preferred by some; but my own favourite of the lot is the ATHENAEUM, for I think its library on the first floor, with its many tall windows, quite the most handsome room in London. The ST. JAMES'S has perhaps the most charming staircase, the SAVAGE the best plaster ceiling and the loveliest view, the GARRICK the best eighteenth-century paintings, and its Byron relics. The SAVILE is a specimen of Edwardian splendour, the AUTOMOBILE CLUB (with so large a membership that it might almost be considered open to the public) the most complete, with its swimming-bath (though the BATH CLUB also boasts one); and the most luxurious is probably the new INTERNATIONAL SPORTSMAN'S CLUB in Grosvenor House. No doubt the vast number of clubs I do not know all have their distinctive charms. Certainly there is a slightly different atmosphere in each club, but just as certainly members are fond of exaggerating the differences, and their similarity and general level are much more striking than their differences. In fact, that rivalry is only another manifestation of the public school and university tradition transferred to another field.

Undoubtedly the men of the younger generation are far less enthusiastic clubmen than their elders; this is partly explained by the fact that the restaurant habit is really comparatively modern in England (there were Victorian *grandes dames* who never entered one in their lives!), and smart hotels are new. Few clubs are as rigidly exclusive as they used to be, and the vision of octogenarians asleep in their easy-chairs is becoming legendary. Gradually clubs are becoming more "frivolous," but I do not think their character will ever change radically. It is most characteristic that modern times have not brought mixed clubs (or very few), but many ladies' clubs, which in their turn only tolerate men, and

106   LORD MAYOR'S DAY

107   CHANGING THE GUARD AT ST JAMES'S PALACE

108   MEDIEVAL FRONTS IN HOLBORN

109   A GEORGIAN FRONT IN THE HAYMARKET

altogether try hard to be as like a male club as possible. Both sexes seem to like their own refuges.

Some of the London shops are as much a part of traditional London as the clubs, and many are to be found in the same neighbourhood. London possesses its huge stores like other capitals: HARROD'S, SELFRIDGE'S, BARKER'S, or WHITELEY'S; other capitals have shops as smart or even smarter in appearance, but what is peculiar to London is that the most famous of famous shops are small, old-fashioned—historical. The English have an immense respect for age and tradition, because these cannot be bought; that is why aristocrats among the shops refuse to compete: they do not advertise either by their exteriors or in any other way—they have no need to. London has, for instance, a number of magnificent modern barbers' shops, full of all the latest improvements, marvellously hygienic, glittering with tiles and nickel and modern lighting effects, heated in winter and cooled in summer. They are to be found in great stores or hotels, and they are also remarkably cheap—but the famous ancient shops have small, old-fashioned premises, no American porcelain chairs, and no splendour of any sort, and a stranger hardly finds his way to them. The grandest barbers of all have no shops, and only serve the favoured few by appointment.

Most of London's historical shops are men's shops; possibly the male sex is the more conservative. One famous place is LOCK'S, the hatshop whose ancient windows merely exhibit a few equally ancient pieces of headgear, possibly made for Nelson or one of the Georges, while the shutters look stout enough to weather many more centuries. Not far from it is BERRY'S, the historic wine-merchants, where generations have done their best to keep hereditary gout alive; while nearly opposite is HOOPER'S, the coachbuilders, surely the last shop left which exhibits broughams and barouches. POOLE'S, the historic tailor of Edwardian fame (when Edward was Prince of Wales), shows a Victorian stucco façade to the world, but really all

R

Savile Row is hallowed by sartorial history. Another famous old shop is FRIBOURG & TREYER'S, the tobacconists in the Haymarket, with its charming old bow-windows, dating from 1720. But apart from such famous shops there are many others in London which, if not famous, certainly deserve to be. There are those distinguished by their fine or quaint architecture, of which there are many in Soho and about Bloomsbury, or hidden in the East End or other poor but old districts; and there are others unique of their kind, such as the house in Grosvenor Road where you will see ship figure-heads exhibited, the wigmaker's shop in the Temple, or a shop for cats' and dogs' meat, all of which could surely not be found in any other capital.

Tradition and history permeate London life in a way unknown in any other great city, and give it its strange charm. You may find tradition alive in small historical cities of many countries, but the capitals have lost it. New York has no past, Paris cut tradition short by the Revolution, Berlin lost its short and Vienna its long tradition in 1918. In London alone the ancient and the modern mingle in the life and appearance of the people as well as in that of the buildings.

It is very characteristic that England alone returned to the old uniforms after the war; so you may see the Horse Guards in Whitehall, so monumentally still upon their horses and beneath their shining cuirasses that you can hardly believe them to be alive; or the changing of the guard, adorned with its huge bearskins, at St. James's, which is so much like one of the later Diaghilev ballets—*a ballet mécanique*. Chelsea has known the red coats of the pensioners since Charles II's time; the Beef-eaters of the Tower have retained Tudor uniform; while on Sundays the Salvation Army flaunts its Victorian bonnets in streets and parks. You will see bluecoat boys in their purely mediaeval clothes in which they can barely walk, and boy scouts, sensibly undressed and picturesque; messenger boys will wear quaint, tiny "pill-box" caps, and the scavengers of Westminster a broad-brimmed Colonial hat. The great football

110 THE OPENING OF THE LAW SESSION: The Judges' Procession from Westminster Abbey

111   SUNDAY IN OXFORD STREET: The Salvation Army

112   SUNDAY IN HYDE PARK: A Jewish Procession

113   THE OPENING OF PARLIAMENT: Peers and Peeresses leaving
the House of Lords

114   AFTER THE CUP FINAL: Football Enthusiasts leaving for the North

115   ROYAL OPENING OF PARLIAMENT

matches will bring green tam-o'-shanters from Ireland or carnival costumes from the North, and fill the West End with cheerful, noisy, and none too sober youths. But on Boat Race night the universities will beat them at their own game, and anything may happen.

The London crowds are as monotonous in dress as those of all cities, since all classes have now adopted the same uniform; but there are still the costermongers in their "pearlies" (one of the prettiest dresses to be found anywhere), though you hardly see them except on the great occasion of the cart-horse parade, and the dilapidatedly picturesque East-Enders of pre-war times have gone. But against the monotony that London shares with other capitals you must set the picturesque pageants and ceremonials it continually provides. Only in London do gilt Baroque coaches still roll through the streets when the Lord Mayor is installed in state or the King and Queen open Parliament, and peers and peeresses appear in their robes of state, looking like the figures of a pack of cards come to life. Not less impressive is the very different ceremony of the Two Minutes' Silence at the Cenotaph on Armistice Day, which shows that the English continue to create new traditions. In London you may see a grave procession of judges in wigs and gowns crossing from the Abbey to Parliament, and all legal life is full of ancient ceremonial. You may meet an ecclesiastical procession complete with choir boys, and learn that they are "beating the bounds" of their parish, and you may even see them doing this in a little boat on the Thames. You may see a meeting of "four-in-hands," and feel you are back in the 'eighties, or notice a crowd around the statue of Charles I, and discover that belated legitimists are still doing him honour, watched over, charmingly if illogically, by the King's Scots Guards.

Another day a crowd will be found collected around a cart in the Borough, for there Dickens is being acted *en plein air,* on the spot where he made his characters lead their lives; or you may find a Negro preaching Christianity to the whites in Hyde Park. If you like ancient ceremonies, you can go and see the boys of Westminster School scrambling for a pancake on Shrove Tuesday, or "Maundy Money," specially minted for that occasion ever since the reign of Edward III, being distributed in leathern purses to as many old men and women as the sovereign can count years on the Thursday before Easter, or oranges and lemons being distributed at St. Clement Danes. You will meet urchins with blackened faces and crackers, because it is Guy Fawkes Day, and they will burn his effigy; you will hear carol-singers in the streets, because it is Christmas, and see Scots massed around St. Paul's on New Year's Eve. On Bank Holidays you will see people marching past to the music of mouth-organs, and Hampstead Heath may convince you that not all the English take their pleasures sadly. One day in the summer you will find London all top-hatted and learn that the Eton and Harrow match takes place that day. Society is always ready to do its share in entertaining the masses, and to sit exposed to the public gaze and comments on its way to levées and Courts, and not many weeks will pass in London without some foreign king or queen arriving, a Chaplin or a Chevalier, an Indian prince or a dusky monarch from Africa. And if there is nothing else, there is sure to be a fashionable wedding, a sight quite peculiar to London, for each wedding is a costume-pageant, a revue scene of flowers and fantastic bridesmaids' garments. You will wonder at the huge crowds these ceremonies attract, chiefly composed of women who seem almost as excited as if it was their own wedding. And any day you will hear the street-organs playing, which have disappeared from the streets of all other capitals, and you may yet hear some of the ancient "cries of London," or meet the muffin-man ringing his bell. But all this is beside and beyond the everyday pageant provided by the life of a city of eight to ten millions—which is the most fascinating of all.

London's year brings an orderly procession of events regulated by tradition, the chief of which is that which

116   LORD MAYOR'S BANQUET AT THE GUILDHALL

117   TENNIS AT WIMBLEDON

118   CRICKET AT LORD'S

119   *L'ALLEGRO*: Bank Holiday on Hampstead Heath

120   *IL PENSEROSO*: Shelling Peas at Covent Garden

121   SATURDAY FOOTBALL CROWD AT STAMFORD BRIDGE

sets apart the "Season" from the rest of the year. Such divisions are innately British, and just as classes and professions are segregated in different districts or streets, so a few months in each year are set apart for all that is gay and brilliant socially. Happily these are the months of spring and early summer, with their outburst of renewed vitality. The Season centres around the Court and its festivities, which means that all connected with it and them must be in town, and the rest follows suit. Society must entertain, give dances and dinners for its debutantes, and everyone who can afford to must be there to attend them. And as "everyone" is in town, then "everything" is there awaiting them. Opera begins, the Academy opens its gates, all the best art shows await patrons. Publishers inundate the market with books, all certified masterpieces; *virtuosi* arrive; first nights abound. Dressmakers and tailors, jewellers and up-holsterers, all the luxury trades get busy; and in the end almost all trades are affected. The streets see a different crowd, the parks are resplendent with flowers; to those who are not actors in the great show every day brings the spectacle of the play proceeding, and they would perhaps resent its abolition more than the actors themselves.

London has to pay for this concentration of gaiety by quiet times, for in August not only Society but the vast masses leave it, while September is quiet, too, though October brings the "Little Season," not officially recog-nised nor as brilliant as the real Season, but in many ways pleasanter, being less of a rush. Christmas brings its traditional festivities, its turkeys and plum puddings, and the pantomimes, those curious stage productions, full of traditional clowning and jokes, and entirely un-connected with what is called a pantomime anywhere else in the world. The early months of the year are perhaps the quietest of all; Society is hunting in the country or has gone abroad; weather and health are poor, London is gloomy, and that is when it is most like what nearly all foreigners who have never seen it imagine it to be all the year round—dark, foggy, splenetic.

S

The Londoner's year is determined far more by sporting events than by the Christian calendar. There are, of course, Christmas and Easter, but the sporting dates are more decisive. There is the football season and the cricket season, *alias* winter and summer. Every Saturday from the last in August to the first in May the matches attract enormous crowds, but the great finals at the end surpass them all. Football is the game of the masses, so it need take no notice of the "Season." The rest of the year means cricket, and here the Eton-Harrow match is the last event of the Season. Its forerunner is the Oxford-Cambridge Boat Race, when the weather is generally cold and nasty, without, however, affecting the enthusiasm. June brings the greatest of all dates, the Derby, a true popular festival, also the Royal Tournament. London is crowded for Ascot—where the smart show off their dresses and the smartest may do this in the Royal Enclosure—the Horse Show, the Aldershot Tattoo, and the Wimbledon tennis tournament, comparatively new but firmly established in the calendar of traditional sport. July brings the Henley Regatta, which has lost something of its former splendour, and the Eton-Harrow match. Then London may rest while Goodwood and Cowes usher in the summer dispersal, and it need not wake again till October brings the Motor Show at Olympia. Thus tradition rules the Londoner's year; its strongest factor is sport, which affects all classes; next comes social distinction, and after that Christianity—or so I think.

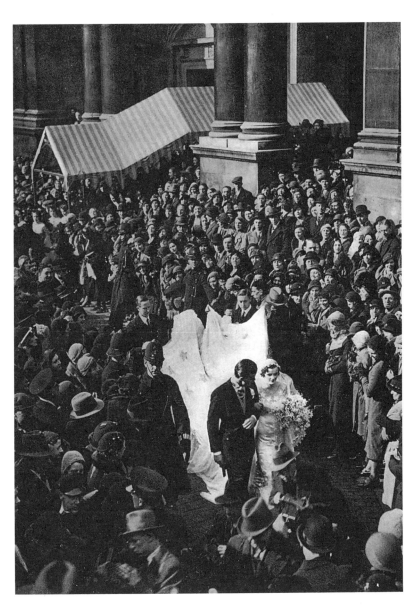

122   ORATORY WEDDING

123, 124   LONDON TRAFFIC

125   LONDON'S AIRPORT, CROYDON

126   A LONDON TERMINUS: Holiday Crowds at Waterloo

127   LONDON'S RIVER: Thames Warehouses, with St Paul's beyond

CHAPTER IX

LONDON AND THE BRITISH

LONDON is the most complex city in the world; to begin with it is a compendium of all the different types of English town. The British are the greatest maritime nation, London is their greatest port, the greatest in the world, New York perhaps excepted. Very important cities, like Hamburg or Marseilles, are proud to be great ports and no more; London is so huge and so varied that one might easily forget or overlook its port and shipping. Probably quite ninety out of every hundred Londoners have never even seen it, for London neglects its river and hides its port. It is a great pity that there should be no regular and efficient steamer service on the Thames, for it is interesting in all its reaches, while there are many sights which can really only be appreciated from the river. What a magnificent procession of architecture and history passes by one: the ecclesiastical palaces of Fulham and Lambeth, Chiswick with its eighteenth-century houses, Chelsea faced by Battersea Park, Westminster, Somerset House, the Temple, St. Paul's cupola, and the Wren spires, and London Bridge, the Tower, shipping, masts and sails and funnels, and on to Greenwich and beyond. It might be London's "Grand Canal," but it is almost inaccessible.

Nor is it possible to get a general impression of the port; there is no huge river-front as at Liverpool or Hamburg, the Docks straggle on both river-banks but do not adjoin each other, and each is enclosed by warehouses, locked and hidden. You must journey to and obtain admission to each separately, and then you may see all the riches of the world piled up on quays or in sombre warehouses: grain and timber, wines and spices, ivory and rubber, skins and carpets, and all the treasure of the East; or if you go to the Victoria and Albert Docks you will find them a huge port in themselves, perhaps the most modern in the world, and you will discover the great liners of the P. and O. and others.

That is one London. But London is also a huge manufacturing city; it is Birmingham or Manchester as well as Liverpool or Southampton, and it manufactures pretty nearly everything. The east and north-east are full of chimneys; but you will find them in the western suburbs, too, and as far as Reading. Next, London is a Cathedral City; you could separate the Abbey and its surroundings from the rest and find a rival to Ely or Wells. It is, of course, many residential towns, so many that one cannot name them. There are austere classical towns (after the manner of Bath), wealthy middle-class towns, cheerful half-rustic settlements like Hampstead, grim proletarian cities like Haxton or Lambeth, and they are all very typically English, for the English are differently housed to continental peoples, and live differently. Abroad, if you except a few modern suburbs, only the very rich have a house of their own; all the others live in flats. But the very rich live in palaces, and London's grandest houses are not palaces like those of Rome or Vienna; the very few which existed have nearly all gone, and the great houses of Mayfair or St. James's are comparatively small and simple, not palaces but large patrician mansions. There is no great gulf between them and those belonging to the wealthy middle-classes, which are very numerous, and, in their turn, much more opulently housed than abroad. The houses show the character and style of life of the people. Even the very large ones, such as you see in Kensington Palace Gardens, Queen's Gate or Lancaster Gate, do not know an enfilade of four or five *salons* and a dining-room to seat a hundred people such as you could find in the expensive flats of pre-war Berlin. On the other hand, you may be sure that there will be a day nursery for the children and a sitting-room, or more than one, for the servants—and these are unknown in continental capitals. In short, the London house is not built for show.

If you consider the moderately wealthy and those of small income, conditions are, I think, immeasurably better in London, for in the suburbs such people can find an endless number of houses with a sufficiency of

128   MILLWALL DOCKS AND THE ISLE OF DOGS, LOOKING TO GREENWICH

129   A RIVERSIDE PUB IN THE EAST END: "The Prospect of
Whitby," Shadwell

130   THE FOREIGNER'S IDEA OF LONDON: Murky Weather
on the Embankment

131   EVENING AT THE PORT OF LONDON

132   DEMOLITION IN STEPNEY

133   RECONSTRUCTION AT THE MARBLE ARCH

rooms, good sanitation, a garden, light, and air. Perhaps to that class the home is more important than to any other, for they mostly spend their evenings there, and in London they can live in a pleasant little house, where abroad they would be crowded in a tiny flat. It is only in such things as central-heating and hot-water supply that the continental flats score; in every other way they are altogether inferior.

But then there are different ways of being happy. A Parisian would think life in a London suburb hopelessly dull, and would much rather put up with a dark and overcrowded small flat and keep the life of the streets and cafés; thus every city expresses the ideals of its people. I think this is true even of the poor and proletarian districts where people have apparently no choice. The slums of all capitals are awful, but awful in a different way, and those of London are quite unlike those of Paris or Berlin, and are as typically English as any other part of the city. They are most depressing, because they are so vast and so mean-looking; they are a maze of small blackened houses, now and again interrupted by a church, a cinema, or a gin-palace. They have none of the picturesqueness of quarters like Belleville or the Faubourg St. Antoine, nor do they hide poverty in a succession of grimy courts behind a bourgeois façade, as in Berlin. But if you consult statistics, you will find far less overcrowding and far better sanitary conditions in London, and that is due to its small houses. Where there are tenements, as in some central districts, the crowding and promiscuity are as abroad, but tenements are few, and it seems difficult to get the poor to live even in new model tenements (an amusing contrast with the new love of flats of the very wealthy). Even the very poor have a touching desire to possess their "own front door," to have a "home." The secret of London is, in fact, that the Londoner, like all Englishmen, is not a creature of cities. He prefers the country, and tries pathetically to live in town as if it were the country. Country means space and solitude, city means crowding and promiscuity; the real town-dweller, the Latin, prefers to live as in a beehive.

T

When you have considered all these different aspects of London, you have still omitted its principal features, which it shares with no other town; they can be indicated by three terms: the City, the Government, the Court—I think I have named them in order of importance. In a sense the City is London, in another it is apart from it. London works in the City and never sees it otherwise. But there it is with its mediaeval topography, Victorian Renascence offices, new white business cliffs, its merchants' halls, and its graceful spires, St. Paul's dominating all. With its ancient traditions and modern bustle, this London is the financial ruler of the British Empire, that is, of one-fourth of humanity, and it has a very large share in the rule of the world. That is where "money" lives, where loans are granted or refused on which the fate of millions depends; this is, in fact, the seat of one of the greatest Powers, if not of the greatest, of the modern world. It has become a symbol, almost a personality; the City thinks. The City is one of the fundamental national institutions, and is what is indispensable to the nation in London—for it might lose its port and its factories and millions of inhabitants without being destroyed, but it would fall to pieces without its City. Almost as inseparable from London as the City, yet not quite, is the Government. Not quite, for one can imagine it being transferred to a "Washington," but it is London's superiority over other capitals that it includes City, Government, and Court. The rule of the City is secret and mysterious; political rule is public: the British world is ruled from Whitehall and Westminster, and here lies Imperial London. It is a city of palaces, white or blackened by age, with the golden grey towers of Westminster in the background. The palaces bear simple names, they are "offices," but they provide plenty of food for the imagination. The Admiralty, old stones and new, looks after the world's greatest navy, the War Office is large, alarmingly large—and the Cenotaph stands near it. How many millions of people will be affected by the decisions taken in that Italianate Foreign Office, how many by what happens in that other huge white palace, the India Office? On this block

134   CITY SPLENDOUR: The Baltic Exchange

135　THE SOUTH SIDE OF THE RIVER: A Wet Afternoon in Vauxhall

136   "THE DOGS": Greyhound Racing at Clapton

137   ONE OF LONDON'S LAST MARKET-PLACES: Cumberland Hay
Market, near Regent's Park

138   A COURT IN SHOREDITCH

depend the colonies, and on that the education of the
rising generation, and from a third emanate budgets
and taxes. Behind them all rises Westminster, with its
Hall where Charles I was condemned to death, to be
executed in Whitehall—an event with which the modern
age began. In the Abbey live all the ages, from early
history to the Great War, and in the Houses of Parliament England's future is decided. Such is London,
the seat of government and parliament, the political ruler
of the British Empire.

And adjoining it "on plan," as it is inseparable from
it in spirit, is the London of the Court, the *Residenzstadt* of
the Court of St. James. I place it last, not because it
is the least important of the three rulers of the Empire—
it is its most important on account of its symbolic
value—but because it is not so indispensable to London.
The Court might decide to reside permanently at
Windsor, just as the Government might transfer its seat
to let us say Bath, and London would still be as important a city as New York, and a more interesting one.
But London is lucky in retaining them, and these are
idle fancies. Here is the "Residency," right in London.
Buckingham Palace and its gardens—a very English
Royal Palace—far less impressive than the palaces of
Berlin, Vienna, Madrid, not to mention the Louvre,
but in the midst of trees and lawns and little hills and
lakes. St. James's Palace is near, set aside for conferences and Court functions, housing the Prince, and the
minor royal residences are not far away. On all sides
stretch the quarters of the important and the rich, and
the nearest is St. James's with its clubs for those who
govern, and provision for all they need—houses, shops,
art treasures, luxury. If one could "cut out" this London
of the Court it would make a second Hague.

That, then, is London of the British: the seat of the
triple rule, Court, Government, and City; the greatest
port, the greatest residential town, a huge factory all in
one. Paris with the addition of Marseilles, Berlin with that
of Hamburg, New York with that of Washington would
yet not attain its completeness; but London resembles
none of them, and is like nothing in the world except itself.

CHAPTER X

LONDON AND THE FOREIGNER

LONDON is one of the world's greatest cosmopolitan cities, but it is cosmopolitan in quite a different manner from the other two great cosmopolitan capitals, Paris and New York. Paris, at least superficially, belongs to the foreigners of all nations almost more than to the French, and if there were no tourists half the city would go bankrupt. New York is continually being invaded by foreigners, if that term has any sense in a city where the vast majority is of non-American parentage. To London its foreigners are not very important, and if they all disappeared things would go on very much the same as before.

There are two sorts of foreigners to be considered, foreign tourists and foreign residents. As to the former, I think there are no available statistics—but London must have extraordinarily few visitors from countries of different language as compared with Paris. Its visitors come from England, from the Dominions and colonies, and many (though far less than go to Paris) from the United States. The Americans are the only foreigners of whom London has taken any notice and who have left their mark upon it. All classes of Americans come here, from the millionaires anxious to entertain Royalty to the schoolmarms who have saved up for years in order to absorb the culture of the Old World. London has adopted American bars and cocktails, soda-fountains (producing rather sickening concoctions, I think), and of course the Hollywood goods. Americans should feel quite at home in the new hotels, flats, or super-cinemas, so largely copied from their own; they will not have to do without their jazz and negro singers, nor will they have any difficulty about paying in dollars. Indeed, they may even find their newspapers sold in the streets, while continentals will miss the newspaper stalls of Paris which cater for all nations, and have some difficulty in discovering the few shops where they can find the papers

they are used to. London has made concession to the
Americans, but they are, after all, half foreign only. Many
of them are, indeed, *plus royalistes que le roi*, and not
altogether pleased with the signs of Americanisation.
They lament every old building that vanishes far more
than do the natives, weep about the new Regent Street,
would like candlelight and Elizabethan beds—in fact,
hoary antiquity to admire, not without a sneaking feeling
of superior modernism.

To other foreign tourists London makes no conces-
sions whatsoever: they must like it or lump it, an attitude I think regrettable. The contrast between the
"Come to Britain" campaign carried on abroad, and
the reception given to foreign tourists when they arrive
is, indeed, extraordinary. England alone of all European
countries subjects visitors to an examination before
allowing them to land, and wishes to know why they
have come, where and how long they are going to stay,
etc. Why this should be necessary I do not know, nor
was it considered so before the war. In any case, visitors
are apt to resent it, and compare it unfavourably with
the friendlier receptions they are accustomed to. Once
in London, they will find themselves rather lost if they
do not speak the language, unless they stay at a big
hotel and never leave it, while Paris or Berlin provide
policemen interpreters. If clever, they will be able to
find the food they are used to, but that is all. They are
used to cafés, but there are none for them; they are used
to "night life," but find themselves sent to bed early,
and they are astounded to find that even an exhibition
closes on Sundays. The West End is open to them and
they may share it with the natives; that is perhaps why
the West End is the least exclusively English part of
London—I mean the West End of theatres and restaurants and shops. There the foreign tourist may feel
welcome, for the shops at least will be glad to see him,
and the shops are London's great atttaction for the
foreign tourist. The men's shops come first of all,
London being the Mecca of all men who think of their
appearance, and next come the Waring's and Maple's,
and the silver and the leather shops. Liberty's, of course,

U

is famous all the world over, as are the shops connected with sport: shops for riding-habits, tennis rackets, mackintoshes, golf clubs. The foreigner new to London will feel at home in the smart hotels and restaurants, so like his own, but not quite at home in the very smartest and the very best, where he will find slightly raised eyebrows if he infringes one of the many un-written laws he has never heard of. He can, of course, see all the wonderful collections and sights, can go to the theatre if he knows the language, but what he cannot do is to enter into the life of the place, for here he will come up against that individualistic English system of segregation and love of privacy, which makes London very pleasant to live in, but is bound to make it chilling to the stranger. Unless he has English friends, for then all will change as if by magic. He will suddenly discover that the Londoners are the most hospitable of people, anxious to do everything to make his stay as pleasant as possible, that doors open far more easily than abroad, that what he thought defects have great compensations. If he may still miss some things he has been used to abroad, he will find many new to him and get to like them. So I would say this: I have hardly ever met a foreign tourist on a short visit to London who has liked it, and I have hardly ever met a foreigner who has lived there for some time who has not loved it. And the only people I have met who know London well and yet do not like it have been English.

But all the same, I think it a pity that so many foreigners should be left to go away with a wrong impression of London and of the English, nor do I think the English attitude logical in this, for if you find foreign visitors undesirable, then you should not encourage their coming by propaganda. If you do this, however, then you should treat them as visitors, not as suspect aliens, and make them welcome. The English character will not change, I know, and to the English the man he does not know does not exist—foreigner or countryman. But there should be an organisation, or several, to look after the visitors. Cities like Berlin or Vienna have their municipal tourist bureaux, where everything is done to facilitate the visitor's stay, while Paris is opening a huge place of a similar sort, the MAISON DE FRANCE. Surely such a thing would be possible in London, too. And if London is a city of clubs, could there not be a foreign tourists' club? No matter what measures are best, some should be taken, in the interests both of the visitors and of London itself.

If the lot of the foreign tourist in London is none too happy, the foreign resident has nothing to complain of, for England is still a most hospitable country, in spite of regulations and supervisions which have come in with the war and remained in force principally on account of the unemployment problem. I do not know the number of foreign residents in London, but it must be colossal, yet they do not play anything like the part they play in Paris—in fact, they play hardly any part at all. The reason for this is not far to seek, for the majority of foreigners in Paris are wealthy: they come to spend money; while the majority of London's foreign residents are poor people: they come to earn money. When the Parisian speaks of an *étranger* he thinks of a man come to Paris to seek pleasure; when the Londoner says "foreigner" he thinks of Italian waiters, Whitechapel Jews, or Chinamen. There are many other foreigners than these living in London, but they disappear in the crowd. The boarding-houses are full of Spaniards, Scandinavians, German young men and girls, over for a year or two to learn English, but they disappear in the English crowd surrounding them. There are many business men, settled in houses in Hampstead or some such place, but they have become anglicised and are lost among their English neighbours; and there are the very rich who take a house on Mayfair for the season. The foreigners of the wealthy classes are submerged in the similar life of the English, and there is no American society or Spanish or South American in London such as you find in Paris.

It is the poor foreigners who are noticeable in London, for their numbers are very great and they congregate in certain districts. They form quarters of their own, and it is these foreign settlements which make London a cosmopolitan city. The Indian students, a class of their own, congregate around Gower Street where they have their club and headquarters; the Chinese live in Limehouse, in disappointingly characterless surroundings. Soho, overflowing into Seven Dials and Charlotte Street, is the Latin centre, Italian and French, or perhaps one should say Mediterranean, for there are many Spaniards, Greeks, Armenians as well, while negroes seem to make Charlotte Street their own. There is another Italian quarter in Clerkenwell, and there may be many other minor foreign settlements that I do not know. The Jews have a peculiar position, as there are British Jews as well as foreign ones. The foreign ones, mostly Russian, live in Whitechapel (and farther east), which is a very ancient Jewish settlement, with old synagogues and burial-grounds; but after a generation or two they become anglicised and disappear in the masses. But all these foreign quarters are as patches, coloured patches, in the huge patchwork quilt that is London, and you could detach them without altering the general pattern much.

I do not think that London will ever be "everyman's city" like Paris, or in a lesser degree Rome or Berlin, but I am not inclined to regret, for this is due to its strong individuality, which to me is the reason of its charm and of its importance. In a world growing more uniform every day, where travelling will soon have ceased to have any object; London has remained a thing apart, different, and with an enormously strong character of its own. That is why it is one of the few cities which should not be missed by any traveller. He may like it or dislike it, but he will have seen something unlike anything else in the world. And if you do like it, its fascination will grow on you; you will never tire of it, because you will never feel you really know it; it is too vast for that, and too complex.

London is a Sphinx and will always remain one: it is moreover a Sphinx continually changing its features and expression. . . . But I hope some of these features and expressions may have been elucidated by this book.

139   A COSMOPOLITAN NEWS-STALL OFF LEICESTER SQUARE

BARGAINS IN DRAPERY AT A LONDON STORE

141, 142   LAW AND ORDER

143   THE TIME, A.D. 1935: Shell House

144   THE TIME, A.D. 1857: "Big Ben"

INDEX

(The numerals in italics denote the *figure-numbers* of illustrations)

X

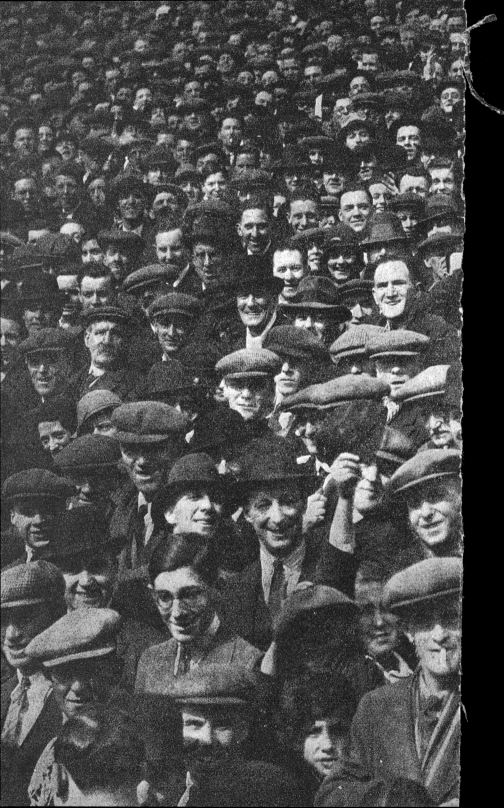